TAKING ROOT

A 7-Week Family Devotional

with Fascinating Facts & Faith-Filled Activities

Amy Hunter

Contents

Welcome!

Thank you so much for choosing this devotional—I'm thrilled that your family is about to take root and grow together! As a homeschooling mom, I've loved starting each day with these reflections and activities, and I hope it brings joy and connection to your family, too. Use it however works best—whether that's going in order, hopping around, or setting your own pace.

While I'm not an authority, I love the Lord and strive to stay faithful to Him. We're all on this journey together, and sometimes we may see things differently—and that's okay! If questions come up, take time to explore the Scriptures together as a family, discussing and praying about any differences. I used the WEBUS translation because it's copyright-free, but feel free to use your favorite version!

Side note: as a self-published author, it's a real challenge to be seen. Reviews help others discover books like this, and I'd be so grateful if you could spare a minute and leave a review. However, if you have feedback feel free to email me at healthyhappyfarm@gmail.com.

Thank you so much for your support, and I pray this devotional will help your family grow in more ways than I can imagine.

God bless you on your journey,

~Amy

CHAPTER 1
CREATION WONDERS

"THE CREATION OF LIGHT"
GUSTAVE DORE'

Day 1

The Beginning of Light

Scripture Spotlight:

"IN THE BEGINNING, GOD CREATED THE HEAVENS AND THE EARTH. THE EARTH WAS FORMLESS AND EMPTY. DARKNESS WAS ON THE SURFACE OF THE DEEP AND GOD'S SPIRIT WAS HOVERING OVER THE SURFACE OF THE WATERS. GOD SAID, 'LET THERE BE LIGHT,' AND THERE WAS LIGHT. GOD SAW THE LIGHT, AND SAW THAT IT WAS GOOD. GOD DIVIDED THE LIGHT FROM THE DARKNESS. GOD CALLED THE LIGHT 'DAY', AND THE DARKNESS HE CALLED 'NIGHT'. THERE WAS EVENING AND THERE WAS MORNING, THE FIRST DAY." - GENESIS 1:1-5

Welcome to the first day of our journey through Creation!

Today, let's illuminate our thoughts and shine a light (pun intended!) on a fascinating topic: light and darkness. As we journey through the creation story, we're not just diving into the physics of light but also uncovering its deeper meanings in our lives.

What Exactly Is Light?

So, what exactly is light anyway? Scientifically speaking, light is more than just a bright bulb or a sunbeam—it's a form of electromagnetic radiation visible to the human eye. It travels through space at an incredible speed of about 186,282 miles per second (299,792 kilometers per second). It's made up of these adorable little packets of energy called photons. These photons pack different energies, giving us the vibrant colors of the rainbow, from radiant reds with long wavelengths to vibrant violets with short wavelengths. And when they all come together, voilà! White light!

Light in Our Lives

And hey, light isn't just about photons and fancy physics. Sometimes, when an idea clicks in our minds, we say a 'lightbulb' went on. Other times, when we're puzzling over something, a helpful explanation can 'light up' our understanding—just like turning on a lamp in a dark room.  Ever had someone swoop in and bring sunshine to your gloomy and dark day? While light can have many meanings, God's light is like no other! Light symbolizes the importance of His presence and guidance in our lives. His light helps us overcome challenges and make good choices. We can follow His light and let it reflect in our lives. Just like light brightens a room, our kindness, love, and positivity can light up someone's day.

Let's Chat:

- Why do we need light in our lives?

- Why do you think God created light on the first day?

Prayer:

Dear God, thank you for the gift of light, both physical and spiritual. Help us to walk in Your light, and use it to guide our steps. Help us to be beacons of Your love and truth, shining brightly in a world that often walks in darkness. Amen.

Fun Fact: The Perfect Design of the Sun and Moon

Isn't it astonishing how perfectly God designed our universe? Take the sun and moon, for instance. Despite their vast differences in size, they are positioned just right relative to each other and to Earth. The sun is about 400 times larger than the moon, but it's also 400 times farther away from us. This perfect balance makes them appear the same size in our sky.

During a solar eclipse, this precise alignment allows the moon to completely cover the sun for a brief, breathtaking moment. The sky darkens during the day, and we get a rare glimpse of the sun's corona, a halo of light that looks like a celestial crown. It's a powerful reminder of God's mastery in creation, perfectly setting each piece in its place for us to witness His glory.

And then there's the moonbow—a nighttime rainbow created by the reflected light of the moon, which is much fainter than sunlight. The delicate balance needed for a moonbow to appear is a reminder of the amazing details and complexities of God's design. Moonbows are rarer and often appear as white arcs, with colors visible on exceptionally dark nights.

These celestial events, both rare and spectacular, remind us of the precision and care God took in crafting our world. As we learn and discuss the wonders of an eclipse or a moonbow, we're reminded of the incredible thought and detail God put into the universe, perfectly aligning everything in His creation.

Creative Corner

MAKE A RAINBOW

Materials Needed:

- A shallow dish or bowl
- A small mirror
- Water
- A flashlight or natural sunlight

Instructions:

✓ Set Up Your Materials: Place the mirror inside the shallow dish or bowl at an angle, leaning against one side so that part of the mirror is submerged under the water.

✓ Add Water: Fill the dish or bowl with water just enough so that half of the mirror is submerged.

✓ Find the Right Light: Position your setup near a sunny window where sunlight can hit the mirror, or use a flashlight if sunlight isn't available. Aim the light source directly at the part of the mirror under the water.

✓ Create Your Rainbow: Adjust the angle of the mirror and the direction of the light until you see a rainbow form on the wall or a surface opposite the light source. The light will reflect off the mirror through the water, dispersing into a spectrum of colors and creating a rainbow.

✓ Experiment: Try changing the angle of the light and the mirror to see how it affects the appearance of the rainbow. See what happens when you move the setup to different locations or use different light sources.

Why did this happen?

When light passes through water, it slows down and bends - a process called refraction. As the light bends, it separates into different colors based on wavelength. The mirror then reflects these colors onto a surface, showing you a rainbow.

Day 2

The Creation of the Sky

Scripture Spotlight:

"GOD SAID, "LET THERE BE AN EXPANSE IN THE MIDDLE OF THE WATERS, AND LET IT DIVIDE THE WATERS FROM THE WATERS." GOD MADE THE EXPANSE, AND DIVIDED THE WATERS WHICH WERE UNDER THE EXPANSE FROM THE WATERS WHICH WERE ABOVE THE EXPANSE; AND IT WAS SO. GOD CALLED THE EXPANSE "SKY". THERE WAS EVENING AND THERE WAS MORNING, A SECOND DAY." - GENESIS 1:6-8

Welcome back, Sky Gazers!

Welcome back to our journey through the *Creation* series. Today, we dive into day two, where God showcases His mastery by artistically separating the waters, creating an expanse known as the sky. As day one brought light out of darkness, day two crafts the skies, setting a divine boundary between the waters above and the waters below.

The Great Divide: Crafting the Sky

Imagine a world where water fills everything above and below. Now, picture God drawing a line, pushing the waters apart to carve out space for the sky. This isn't just about moving water around; it's about designing a perfect home for all of us. This

act of separation sets the stage for life as we know it, introducing order and structure to our universe.

The Sky: Our Protective Blanket

Think of the sky as Earth's superhero shield! It guards us against the harshness of outer space, regulates our climate, and filters out harmful radiation from the sun. Without this protective canopy, Earth would be a lot like a house without a roof!

Water: The Source of Life

Covering about 71% of the Earth's surface, water is more than just something to drink—it's the lifeline for all living things. By separating the waters, God ensured that life could thrive on Earth, showing incredible foresight and care for His creation.

Spiritual Hydration: A Drink from Jesus

Water refreshes our bodies, but our spirits need hydration too. Jesus offers us 'living water'—a kind of water that quenches our deepest thirsts forever. Think about how water is essential for life, and how Jesus' offer of spiritual water is essential for our souls.

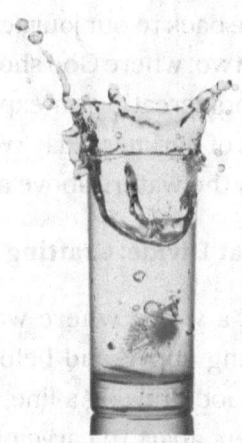

Let's Chat:

- When have you noticed that setting a boundary or separating something made things better?

- Why do you think boundaries are important?

Prayer:

Dear God, thank you for the beauty of separation and unity. Guide us in understanding the purpose of boundaries and separations in our lives. Please help us appreciate the order they bring while cherishing the connections they allow. Amen.

Fun Fact: Waterworks

Most liquids contract when they freeze, but water behaves uniquely—it expands as it freezes, becoming less dense than its liquid form. This unusual property is why ice floats on water. Without it, bodies of water would freeze from the bottom up, posing severe challenges for aquatic life in colder climates.

Speaking of freezing, have you heard of the Mpemba effect? It's a curious phenomenon where hot water can sometimes freeze faster than cold water. Intrigued? Try this experiment to see it in action: Freeze a cup of cold water alongside a cup of boiling water (be careful not to burn yourself!). Keep an eye on them and you might be surprised to see which one freezes first!

Creative Corner

MAKE A LAVA LAMP

Materials Needed:

- A clear, transparent bottle or glass (an empty water bottle or mason jar works well)
- Vegetable or baby oil
- Water
- Food coloring (optional for added visual effect)
- Alka-Seltzer or similar effervescent tablets

Instructions:

✓ Add Oil: Fill your bottle or glass about three-quarters full with oil.

✓ Add Water: Pour water into the bottle, leaving about one-quarter of the bottle unfilled.

✓ Add Food Coloring (Optional): Add a few drops for a visual effect.

✓ Watch the Separation: Observe how the water settles at the bottom of the bottle while the oil stays on top, due to their different densities.

✓ Create the "Lava Lamp" Effect: Break an effervescent tablet into smaller pieces.

✓ Drop one piece into the bottle and watch as it reacts with the water, creating bubbles that rise through the oil layer.

✓ Enjoy the Show: The bubbles carry droplets of water with them as they rise to the top of the bottle. As the bubbles pop at the surface, the water droplets fall back down due to their density, creating a mesmerizing effect.

BONUS ACTIVITY: WITNESS THE WATER CYCLE!

Materials Needed:
- A shallow dish of water
- A heat source (like a lamp or sunlight)
- Clear plastic wrap
- A small weight (like a rock)

1. Place the dish of water under a lamp or in direct sunlight to warm the water.
2. Cover the dish with clear plastic wrap and place the small weight in the center.
3. Watch as the water evaporates and condenses on the plastic wrap, resembling the water cycle. This demonstration shows how water evaporates, forms clouds, and precipitates- reflecting the separation of waters as described in Genesis.

Day 3

The Emergence of Land, Seas, and Plants

Scripture Spotlight:

"GOD SAID, 'LET THE WATERS UNDER THE SKY BE GATHERED
TOGETHER TO ONE PLACE, AND LET THE DRY LAND APPEAR;'
AND IT WAS SO. GOD CALLED THE DRY LAND 'EARTH', AND THE
GATHERING TOGETHER OF THE WATERS HE CALLED 'SEAS'. GOD
SAW THAT IT WAS GOOD. GOD SAID, 'LET THE EARTH YIELD
GRASS, HERBS YIELDING SEEDS, AND FRUIT TREES BEARING
FRUIT AFTER THEIR KIND, WITH THEIR SEEDS IN IT, ON THE
EARTH;' AND IT WAS SO. THE EARTH YIELDED GRASS, HERBS
YIELDING SEED AFTER THEIR KIND, AND TREES BEARING FRUIT,
WITH THEIR SEEDS IN IT, AFTER THEIR KIND; AND GOD SAW

THAT IT WAS GOOD. THERE WAS EVENING AND THERE WAS MORNING, A THIRD DAY." - GENESIS 1:9-13

Ahoy, Explorers of Creation!

In today's journey through *Creation*, we witness the spectacular emergence of land, seas, and vibrant plant life! Building on the theme of separation established on Days One and Two, Day Three brings about another miraculous division—this time preparing Earth for the abundant life that is to follow. Imagine the excitement of seeing dry land appear for the first time, separating from the waters and forming mountains, valleys, and plains. Picture the earth being covered with lush green grass, vibrant herbs, and towering trees, each one unique and beautiful in its own way.

The Appearance of Land:

In a grand act of creation, God gathered the waters and revealed the dry land, calling it "earth." The vast seas were formed, teeming with potential for life. This separation of land and water set the stage for all living things to thrive. It's like watching a master architect start a breathtaking landscape project, with each structure coming together to form ponds, hills, and rocks, adding more beauty and detail.

The Green Carpet Unrolls:

 God didn't stop there! He commanded the earth to produce vegetation: grass that carpets the ground, herbs yielding seeds, and fruit trees bearing delicious fruits. Imagine the first apple tree bursting into bloom, the first fields of wheat swaying in the breeze, and the first flowers adding brilliant colors to the world. These plants weren't just pretty to look at—they were essential for life, providing food and oxygen through the remarkable process of photosynthesis.

God's Perfect Plan

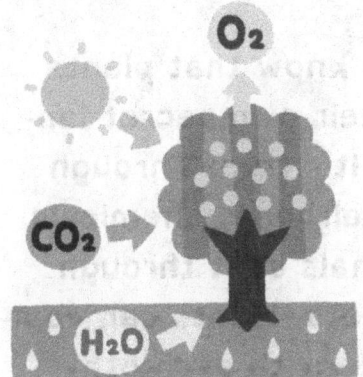

Every plant was created with a purpose. Grass provides food for animals, herbs offer nourishment and medicine, and fruit trees give us sweet, sustaining treats. Plus, plants produce the oxygen we need to breathe! God's design is unbelievably intricate and perfect, showing His care and wisdom in every detail.

Growth in Our Lives

Just as plants need water and light to grow, we need God's living water and His light in our lives to flourish. Jesus said, "I am the light of the world" (John 8:12), and He offers us living water that satisfies our deepest needs (John 4:14). By reading, listening, and applying His words from the Bible to our daily lives, we will continue to grow and flourish according to His will.

Let's Chat:

- Would you rather live near a river or an ocean? Why?

- Would you rather climb a mountain or hike in the desert? Why?

Prayer:

Dear God, thank you for the beauty of the land, seas, and plants you crafted on Day Three. May we cherish the wonders around us and grow the way You intended us to. In Jesus' name. Amen.

Fun Fact: Plants Talk Too!

Did you know that plants have their own secret language? It's true! Through special airborne chemicals and signals sent through their roots, plants can communicate with each other. They share warnings about dangers like pests or changes in their environment, almost like sending a message to a friend.

For example, when a plant is attacked by insects, it can release chemicals to alert nearby plants to produce their own protective chemicals. This amazing botanical dialogue helps plants support and protect each other.

So next time you see plants swaying in the breeze, remember that they might be having a chat about how to stay safe and healthy. Now that's what I call being a good neighbor!

Creative Corner

CELEBRATING GOD'S CREATION WITH A RECIPE!

Inspired by Day 3's creation of vegetation, which provides sustenance for all life, we can celebrate with recipes that reflect the earth's bounty.
Enjoy making a Chickpea and Herb Salad or a Simple Fruit Smoothie, using fresh ingredients that remind us of God's generous provision.

CHICKPEA AND HERB SALAD

Ingredients:

- 1 can (15 oz) chickpeas
- 1 small red onion
- 1 cucumber
- 1 tomato
- Fresh parsley, fresh mint, or salad greens
- Lemon juice
- Extra-virgin olive oil
- Salt, and pepper

Instructions:

- Rinse and drain chickpeas; pat dry.
- In a bowl, combine chickpeas, chopped onion, diced cucumber, diced tomato, parsley, mint, and salad greens.
- Dress it up with a splash of lemon juice, olive oil, salt, and pepper; toss to combine.
- Serve and enjoy this refreshing, nutritious snack.

SIMPLE FRUIT SMOOTHIE

Ingredients:

- 1 ripe banana
- 1 cup frozen berries
- 1 cup milk or juice
- Optional: nut butter, chia seeds, flaxseeds, sweetener.

Instructions:

- Blend all ingredients until smooth.
- Enjoy immediately for a delicious and healthy treat!

Day 4

Day 4: Illuminating the Heavens

Scripture Spotlight:

"GOD SAID, "LET THERE BE LIGHTS IN THE EXPANSE OF THE SKY TO DIVIDE THE DAY FROM THE NIGHT; AND LET THEM BE FOR SIGNS TO MARK SEASONS, DAYS, AND YEARS; AND LET THEM BE FOR LIGHTS IN THE EXPANSE OF THE SKY TO GIVE LIGHT ON THE EARTH;" AND IT WAS SO. GOD MADE THE TWO GREAT LIGHTS: THE GREATER LIGHT TO RULE THE DAY, AND THE LESSER LIGHT TO RULE THE NIGHT. HE ALSO MADE THE STARS. GOD SET THEM IN THE EXPANSE OF THE SKY TO GIVE LIGHT TO THE EARTH, AND TO RULE OVER THE DAY AND OVER THE NIGHT, AND TO DIVIDE THE LIGHT FROM THE DARKNESS. GOD SAW THAT IT WAS GOOD. THERE WAS EVENING AND THERE WAS MORNING, A FOURTH DAY." – GENESIS 1:14-19

Welcome, Cosmic Time-Travelers!

Hey there, cosmic time-travelers! Brace yourselves as we launch into the wonders of Day Four in our journey through *Creation*. Today, God unveils the grandeur of space and time through the creation of the sun, moon, and stars.

Guiding Lights of the Universe:

As we turn our gaze to the heavens, we see not just ornaments in the sky but guiding lights across the heavenly expanse. While the vastness of the universe humbles us, it reminds us of our small yet significant place in God's grand design.

The Reigning Luminaries:

God appointed the sun and moon as the reigning luminaries of Earth. The sun does more than illuminate; it provides essential light, warmth, and energy. Meanwhile, the moon, as it orbits around Earth, causes different portions of its sunlit side to be visible. This ever-changing appearance, known as a phase, not only enhances the beauty of the night sky but also teaches us about the moon's significant role beyond its glow. Its gravitational pull is powerful enough to influence Earth's tides, affecting the natural rhythm of our oceans.

The North Star:

Additionally, the stars in the heavens play pivotal roles in many of our cherished biblical stories, none more famous than the Star of Bethlehem. As told in Matthew 2:1-2, "After Jesus was born in Bethlehem in Judea, during the time of King Herod, Magi from the east came to Jerusalem and asked, 'Where is the one who has been born king of the Jews? We saw his star when it rose and have come to worship him.'" This star, also known as the North Star, didn't just guide the Wise Men geographically but also signified the birth of Jesus, heralding a new era and the arrival of the Light of the World. The stars, set in place on the fourth day of creation, serve not only to light our nights and mark the seasons but also to fulfill profound prophetic roles in God's redemptive plan.

Let's Chat:

- How do you think the stars help us tell time?

- How do the seasons influence your family's activities or traditions?

Prayer:

Heavenly Father, we thank You for the sun, moon, and stars—the heavenly bodies that bring light to our lives. As we observe the changing seasons and gaze upon the night sky, help us to truly appreciate the splendor of Your creation. May we find joy and wonder in every sunrise, sunset, and starlit night. In Jesus' name, Amen.

Fun Fact: Super Star!

According to NASA, Neutron stars are incredibly dense remnants of massive stars that have undergone supernova explosions. They are said to be so dense that a teaspoon of their material would weigh billions of tons on Earth!

But get this, some of these neutron stars, known as pulsars, can rotate at astonishing rates, ranging from milliseconds to a few seconds per revolution. Imagine a star the size of a city spinning faster than a kitchen blender!

Creative Corner

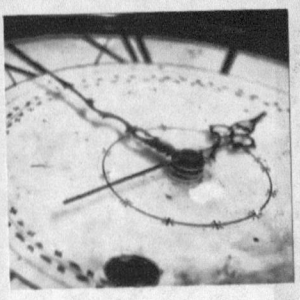

DIY SUNDIAL

As we explore the creation of the sun, moon, and stars on Day 4, which serve as timekeepers, let's create our own timepiece. Follow these steps to make a Sundial, an ancient method of measuring time using the sun's position in the sky.

Instructions:

Materials Needed:

- A flat, horizontal surface (a sunny outdoor space)
- A stick (about 12 inches or 30 cm long)
- Small pebbles or rocks
- A clock or watch

 1. Choose a sunny day to do this activity.

 2. Find a flat, open outdoor space where the sun will be visible for most of the day.

 3. Insert the stick vertically into the ground, ensuring it stands upright and doesn't wobble.

 4. Place small pebbles or rocks around the base of the stick to mark the hours on the clock (1:00, 2:00, etc.). You can estimate the positions based on the shadow cast by the stick.

 5. Observe the shadow cast by the stick and the current time on your clock or watch.

 6. Adjust the position of the rocks or pebbles as the day progresses, keeping track of the changing shadow.

Day 5

The Splendor of Sea and Sky

Scripture Spotlight:

"GOD SAID, "LET THE WATERS ABOUND WITH LIVING CREA-
TURES, AND LET BIRDS FLY ABOVE THE EARTH IN THE OPEN EX-
PANSE OF THE SKY." GOD CREATED THE LARGE SEA CREATURES
AND EVERY LIVING CREATURE THAT MOVES, WITH WHICH THE
WATERS SWARMED, AFTER THEIR KIND, AND EVERY WINGED
BIRD AFTER ITS KIND. GOD SAW THAT IT WAS GOOD. GOD
BLESSED THEM, SAYING, "BE FRUITFUL, AND MULTIPLY, AND
FILL THE WATERS IN THE SEAS, AND LET BIRDS MULTIPLY ON
THE EARTH." THERE WAS EVENING AND THERE WAS MORNING,
A FIFTH DAY." - GENESIS 1:20-23

Welcome Back, Explorers!

Today, we plunge into the depths of Day Five, where God fills everything from the deepest part of the ocean to the heights of the skies with an incredible array of creatures.

Dive into the Depths:

Imagine the underwater world God created, bustling with a variety of fish, turtles, sharks, jellyfish, clams, and more. The diversity and wonder of aquatic life are beyond what we can fully comprehend. Even today, the deepest parts of the ocean, like the Challenger Deep at over 36,000 feet, remain largely unexplored, a testament to the vastness of God's creations.

Birds of the Sky:

Looking upwards, we see birds soaring, dancing, and singing, showcasing God's brilliance in flight. From the rapid hummingbird fluttering its wings over 50 times per second to the albatross that glides for hours, the sky is filled with a symphony of movements that reflect divine choreography.

Creation's Harmony:

Both the sea and sky are filled with life, with each creature perfectly fit for its environment. This day reminds us of God's intention for harmony and beauty in all things. From the colorful coral reefs to the majestic eagles, each element of creation has a role that contributes to the ecosystem's health and vibrancy. The vast variety of sea and sky creatures reveal the boundless creativity of our Creator. Each creature is unique and shows us God's incredible design and the care He has for every detail.

Let's Chat:

- Why do you think God created creatures in the sea and birds in the sky on the same day?

- What's your favorite sea creature, and why? Is it its appearance, behavior, habitat, or something else entirely?

Prayer:

Dear Lord, thank you for the beauty of the land, seas, and skies you crafted on Day Five. As we marvel at the diversity and complexity of your creations, help us to appreciate and care for your wonderful world. Amen.

Fun Fact: Mantis Shrimp's Dual Superpowers!

 Mantis shrimp are not just ordinary sea creatures; they are underwater superheroes! Their club or spear-like appendages strike with lightning-fast speed, creating shockwaves that can stun or even kill their prey instantly. Picture that! What's more, mantis shrimp have the ability to move their eyes independently and possess unparalleled eyesight. While humans have only three types of color-receptive cones, mantis shrimp flaunt over twelve types, allowing them to perceive a spectrum of colors way beyond ours. Let that sink in!

Creative Corner

MAKE A BIRD FEEDER

Want to attract some feathered friends?
Try one of these easy bird feeder activities:

PEANUT BUTTER PINECONE BIRD FEEDER

Materials:
- Pinecones
- Peanut butter or suet
- Birdseed
- String
- Alternative: Clean, empty paper towel or toilet paper roll

Instructions:
1. Tie a piece of string around the top of the pinecone to create a loop for hanging.
2. Generously spread peanut butter or suet over the pinecone, filling the crevices.
3. Roll the pinecone in birdseed, ensuring it sticks to the peanut butter or suet.
4. Hang the pinecone feeder on a tree branch and watch the birds flock for a feast!

GELATIN COOKIE CUTTER BIRD FEEDER

Materials:
- Birdseed
- Gelatin (unflavored)
- Cookie cutters
- Drinking straws (for holes)
- String
- Tray lined with parchment paper

Instructions:
1. Prepare the gelatin according to package instructions with hot water.
2. Stir in the birdseed until well coated.
3. Place cookie cutters on the lined tray and fill them with the birdseed mixture.
4. Insert a straw into each filled cutter to create a hole for hanging.
5. Let the mixture solidify in the fridge.
6. Once firm, remove the feeders from the cookie cutters, remove the straws, and thread string through the holes.
7. Hang these delightful shaped feeders around your yard and enjoy watching the birds visit.

Day 6

The Dawn of Life on Land

Scripture Spotlight:

"GOD SAID, "LET THE EARTH PRODUCE LIVING CREATURES AFTER THEIR KIND, LIVESTOCK, CREEPING THINGS, AND ANIMALS OF THE EARTH AFTER THEIR KIND;" AND IT WAS SO. GOD MADE THE ANIMALS OF THE EARTH AFTER THEIR KIND, AND THE LIVESTOCK AFTER THEIR KIND, AND EVERYTHING THAT CREEPS ON THE GROUND AFTER ITS KIND. GOD SAW THAT IT WAS GOOD. GOD SAID, "LET'S MAKE MAN IN OUR IMAGE, AFTER OUR LIKENESS. LET THEM HAVE DOMINION OVER THE FISH OF THE SEA, AND OVER THE BIRDS OF THE SKY, AND OVER THE LIVESTOCK, AND OVER ALL THE EARTH, AND OVER EVERY CREEPING THING THAT CREEPS ON THE EARTH." GOD CREATED MAN IN HIS OWN IMAGE. IN GOD'S IMAGE HE CREATED HIM; MALE AND FEMALE HE CREATED THEM. GOD BLESSED THEM.

GOD SAID TO THEM, "BE FRUITFUL, MULTIPLY, FILL THE EARTH, AND SUBDUE IT. HAVE DOMINION OVER THE FISH OF THE SEA, OVER THE BIRDS OF THE SKY, AND OVER EVERY LIVING THING THAT MOVES ON THE EARTH." GOD SAID, "BEHOLD, I HAVE GIVEN YOU EVERY HERB YIELDING SEED, WHICH IS ON THE SURFACE OF ALL THE EARTH, AND EVERY TREE, WHICH BEARS FRUIT YIELDING SEED. IT WILL BE YOUR FOOD. TO EVERY ANIMAL OF THE EARTH, AND TO EVERY BIRD OF THE SKY, AND TO EVERYTHING THAT CREEPS ON THE EARTH, IN WHICH THERE IS LIFE, I HAVE GIVEN EVERY GREEN HERB FOR FOOD;" AND IT WAS SO. GOD SAW EVERYTHING THAT HE HAD MADE, AND, BEHOLD, IT WAS VERY GOOD. THERE WAS EVENING AND THERE WAS MORNING, A SIXTH DAY." - GENESIS 1:24-31

Welcome to the Parade!

On the wild and wonderful sixth day of *Creation*, God unleashed a parade of amazing creatures—from graceful gazelles to quirky quokkas, creepy crawling caterpillars to lounging lizards, and everything in between.

Each one is an unbelievable masterpiece! Now, on this day, we can envision a lit-up world teeming with vibrant plant life, where birds soar through the skies, fish dance in the ocean depths, animals graze on the ground, and creepy crawlers climb on tree limbs. God's greatness shines through it all!

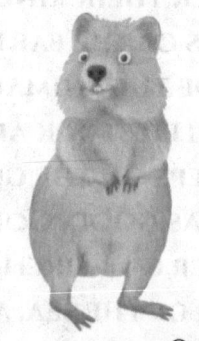

Quokka

A Special Creation:

But hold on, the day isn't over yet! After crafting this brilliant array of creatures, God decided to create something truly special to Him. He fashioned humans in His image to rule over all the Earth.

Divine Masterpieces:

Yes, you read that right—we're not just another creature; we're divine masterpieces, meticulously sculpted and designed to reflect God's image. He didn't make us for mere amusement either. No, He had a purpose, a unique job for us. He entrusted us with the responsibility to have dominion over the Earth, to protect, manage, and care for His incredible creation.

Stewardship and Community:

Now, if you're thinking, "I can hardly take care of my room," don't worry. God always has a plan. When He said, "Be fruitful, multiply, fill the Earth, and subdue it," He made it clear that He didn't want us to manage everything by ourselves. He wanted us to care for His creation as a family. By the way, did you notice what the Bible says at the end of day 6? It says,

"God saw everything that He had made, and behold, it was very good." He was very pleased with His creation.

Our Role:

As we celebrate the gift and privilege of day six, let's remember that we're God's image-bearers, called to reflect Him and care for His amazing world. Whether you're outside marveling at the sky, observing majestic creatures, or relating to family members (even when it's tough!), remember that God lovingly crafted everything you see. He has a special role for each of us in this incredible adventure!

Let's Chat:

- What's your favorite animal created on Day 6 and why?

- How does understanding that we are made in God's image influence our interactions with the world and each other?

Prayer:

Dear Heavenly Father, as we contemplate Your marvelous creation, please open our eyes to the wonders of Your handiwork. Thank you for entrusting us as stewards of this beautiful earth. Please guide us to live wisely and compassionately, reflecting Your image in all that we do. Amen.

Fun Fact: God's DNA Masterpiece

Did you know that inside your body, there's an epic DNA adventure? Your body is like a bustling city with 37.2 trillion cells, each carrying a tiny copy of your DNA. If you stretched out all this DNA from one person, it would reach from Earth to the Sun and back multiple times! This mind-boggling complexity highlights God's extraordinary craftsmanship.

DNA is like God's secret code, containing all the information needed to build and maintain your body. It's your unique recipe book. So, when you look in the mirror, remember you're not just seeing yourself; you're gazing at a masterpiece of God's design, a living, breathing work of art, and part of the incredible story of creation.

Creative Corner

MAKE A FAMILY PORTRAIT

Materials Needed:

- Paint, pencils, markers, or crayons
- Paper

Instructions:

1. Draw your family!
2. Identify and write down the great qualities within your family that mirror the image of God. Consider traits like kindness, forgiveness, gentleness, patience, faithfulness, and generosity.

ALTERNATIVE ACTIVITY: SHADOW ART

Materials:

- Large sheet of white paper or poster board
- Pencil
- Lamp or light source
- Tape

Instructions:

1. **Choose a Wall:** Find a flat, well-lit wall where you can set up your materials.
2. **Position the Light:** Set up a lamp or light source on one side, casting a strong shadow against the wall. Make sure the light is at a good angle to create a clear and defined shadow.
3. **Stand or Sit:** Position yourself between the light source and the wall. Decide on a pose for your self-portrait, whether it's standing, sitting, or a unique pose.
4. **Trace the Shadow:** Have someone else trace your shadow on the wall using a pencil. Alternatively, you can tape the paper to the wall and trace your own shadow.
5. **Add Details:** Once the basic outline is traced, you can add details to make it more personalized. Outline your facial features, hair, and clothing. Get creative with the details!
6. **Cut Out the Portrait:** Carefully cut along the traced lines to create your shadow self-portrait.
7. **Mount or Display:** Tape or mount your cut-out self-portrait onto another piece of paper or poster board for stability. You can also add a background or decorate the surrounding area.

Day 7

A Day Of Rest

Scripture Spotlight:

"THE HEAVENS, THE EARTH, AND ALL THEIR VAST ARRAY WERE FINISHED. ON THE SEVENTH DAY GOD FINISHED HIS WORK WHICH HE HAD DONE; AND HE RESTED ON THE SEVENTH DAY FROM ALL HIS WORK WHICH HE HAD DONE. GOD BLESSED THE SEVENTH DAY, AND MADE IT HOLY, BECAUSE HE RESTED IN IT FROM ALL HIS WORK OF CREATION WHICH HE HAD DONE." - GENESIS 2:1-3

Greetings, Adventurers! Let's Take a Break!

Welcome to the seventh day of *Creation!* On this day, something truly extraordinary happened—God rested. He didn't rest because He was tired; rather, He rested because His work was complete. Think about it this way: Have you ever created a piece of artwork, something very special, with time and care? When you finally finish it, what do you do? You don't just put it aside, do you? No, you stop working and take a moment to admire it. Maybe you display it for a while to enjoy your finished masterpiece. Similarly, God rested after He declared His work 'very good,' and He blessed the day and made it holy.

The Sabbath: A Day Set Apart:

The seventh day, known as the Sabbath, sets an example for us to follow. In the Ten Commandments, we are reminded that on this holy day, no one should be working (Exodus 20:8). Furthermore, Jesus teaches us in Mark 2:24-28 that God gave us the Sabbath day as a gift. By setting aside this day, God invites us to step away from the busyness of life and work and to focus on what truly matters.

A Time for Reflection:

On this special day, we can cherish and appreciate the gift of rest and reflect on God's love for us. It's a precious time to recharge and spend quality moments with God. One way to celebrate this day as a family is to set aside time to worship, pray, and read the Bible together. Sharing stories of God's goodness and creating joyful traditions is another way we can celebrate. Let's remember to rejoice and be glad in the beauty of His creation, just as God did on the seventh day.

Let's Chat:

- How is day seven different from days one through six of creation?
- Why do you think it's important to rest?

Prayer:

Dear Heavenly Father, Thank you for the beauty and completeness of Your creation. As we reflect on the seventh day, help us find rest in Your perfect plan for our lives. Teach us to trust You even when things seem uncertain, and remind us to take the gift of rest that You've given us. In our moments of rest and reflection, may we follow You and find peace in Your presence. Amen.

Fun Fact: The Power of Breaks and Days Off

<u>The Brain-Boosting Benefits of Rest:</u>
Did you know taking breaks and
having a day off from work can
actually supercharge your brain?

 When we step away from our usual
tasks, our brains can recharge and
explore new ideas and connections.
It's like giving your mind a mini-va-
cation. It isn't just refreshing—it enhances creativity and productivity.

<u>Health Risks of Skipping Rest:</u> But
wait, there's more! Consistently skipping breaks can really put a damper
on your health. Imagine running a
marathon without any water breaks—it can lead
to a higher risk of issues like heart disease, anx-
iety, and other health complications. Taking that
much-needed break is like hitting the "refresh"
button. And guess what? God knew exactly what
He was doing when He instituted the Sabbath. We
need it to keep our bodies in tip-top shape and
enjoy the journey of life fully!

Creative Corner

ADVENTURE IN GODS'S CREATION!

Get ready to step into a world of wonder and beauty —right in your own backyard or local park!

Plan and go on a family adventure into the heart of nature. As you stroll through the woods or park, take a moment to observe and discuss how every leaf, bird, and breeze speaks of God's meticulous design.

Fun Things To Do:

1. Gear Up for Discovery: Grab your explorer hats and binoculars if you have them, and lace up your walking shoes! Bring along a notebook or a camera to capture and jot down the marvels you encounter.
2. Scavenger Hunt Challenge: Turn your walk into a thrilling scavenger hunt! Make a list of natural items to find, such as a certain type of leaf, an insect, a bird, and something mysterious or unexpected. Who can spot their items first?
3. Creative Captures: Use your camera or phone to take photos of interesting plants, animals, or landscapes.
4. Reflect and Sketch: Bring sketchpads and pencils. Pause at a scenic spot to draw what you see or feel. It could be a leafy tree, a serene pond, or a busy squirrel. Expressing your observations through art can be a peaceful and reflective activity.

ALTERNATIVE ACTIVITY: START A SABBATH DAY TRADITION

Transform your Sabbath into a day of rest, reflection, and family bonding with a special tradition. Here are a few inspiring ideas:

1. Nature Walk: Take a leisurely walk together and share the wonders you witness, discussing how each element of nature reflects God's perfect plan and creativity.
2. Special Meal: Prepare a meal inspired by the beauty of creation and enjoy it together, appreciating the abundance God provides.
3. Storytelling or Reading: Spend quiet time storytelling or reading.
4. Creative Activities: Create art or craft projects that reflect the beauty of God's handiwork, creating lasting memories and expressions of thanks.

CHAPTER 2
AMAZING BIBLICAL CREATURES
A Closer Look at Some of God's Most Jaw-Dropping Creations

Day 1

The Leviathan: A Dragon of the Deep!

Scripture Spotlight:

"CAN YOU DRAW OUT LEVIATHAN WITH A FISH HOOK, OR PRESS DOWN HIS TONGUE WITH A CORD? CAN YOU PUT A ROPE INTO HIS NOSE, OR PIERCE HIS JAW THROUGH WITH A HOOK?" - JOB 41:1-2

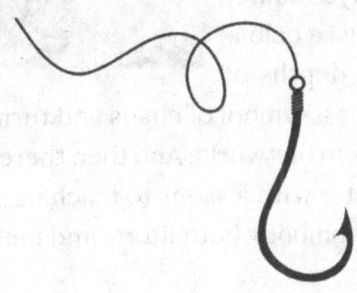

Welcome to the Fascinating Realm of Biblical Creatures:

As we begin the second chapter of our family devotional, we set our sails on an exciting journey to uncover the mysteries of amazing creatures mentioned in the Bible. From the depths of the sea to the skies above, these creatures reveal the majesty and creativity of our God. Let's begin with the awe-inspiring Leviathan!

Dive into the Depths:

Enter the captivating tale of the Leviathan, a creature so magnificent and awe-inspiring, it leaps straight from the pages of Job 41 into our wildest imaginations. Picture this: a gargantuan sea beast with armor-like skin no weapon can pierce, fearsome teeth ready to snap, and the ability to breathe fire. Yes, you heard that right—fire! It's like something out of a fantasy novel, but it's not, it's our very own biblical dragon.

In fact, in the Septuagint—the ancient Greek translation of the Old Testament—the word for Leviathan is translated as "drakon," which is the Greek word for "dragon." How cool is that?

A Creature of Many Tales:

The Leviathan has fascinated people across history and cultures, sparking a spectrum of beliefs. Some envision it as a real creature that once ruled the waters, maybe something like the Deinosuchus, a colossal crocodilian from the depths of  prehistory. Others see it as a symbol of chaos and turmoil, a representation of the untamed forces in our world. And then there are those who see it as both: a real sea monster with lessons to teach us, much like how the words snake and monster embody both literal and metaphorical threats.

The Twist in the Tale:

While the Leviathan might be a nightmarish beast, it also shows us just how powerful our God is. Even the most fearsome creature in the imagination of humanity pales in comparison to the Creator's power. We read that Job was humbled and awestruck as he learned that there is nothing too vast or daunting for God to handle.

The Treasure Trove:

So, as we journey through the Bible and encounter stories like that of the Leviathan, let's marvel not at the creature but at the Creator. For there is nothing too great, too fearsome, or too powerful for our God. He's the ultimate hero of every story, the King above all kings, and nothing can compare. Today, let's sit on that truth, holding onto the awe-inspiring power of God, knowing there's absolutely nothing beyond His reach.

Additional Scriptures:

JOB 3:8: "LET THEM CURSE IT WHO CURSE THE DAY, WHO ARE READY TO ROUSE UP LEVIATHAN."

JOB 41:1-2: "CAN YOU DRAW OUT LEVIATHAN WITH A FISH HOOK, OR PRESS DOWN HIS TONGUE WITH A CORD? CAN YOU PUT A ROPE INTO HIS NOSE, OR PIERCE HIS JAW THROUGH WITH A HOOK?"

PSALM 74:14: "YOU BROKE THE HEADS OF LEVIATHAN IN PIECES. YOU GAVE HIM AS FOOD TO PEOPLE AND DESERT CREATURES."

PSALM 104:25-26: "THERE IS THE SEA, GREAT AND WIDE, IN WHICH ARE INNUMERABLE LIVING THINGS, BOTH SMALL AND

LARGE ANIMALS. THERE THE SHIPS GO, AND LEVIATHAN, WHOM YOU FORMED TO PLAY THERE."

ISAIAH 27:1: "IN THAT DAY, YAHWEH WITH HIS HARD AND GREAT AND STRONG SWORD WILL PUNISH LEVIATHAN, THE FLEEING SERPENT, AND LEVIATHAN, THE TWISTED SERPENT; AND HE WILL KILL THE DRAGON THAT IS IN THE SEA."

Let's Chat:

- What do you think it would be like to see the Leviathan up close?
- How does knowing God is even more powerful than the Leviathan help you face your own 'monsters'?

Fun Fact Discovering the Deinosuchus:

Imagine stumbling upon a creature with teeth as long as bananas and measuring nearly 40 feet long. Meet Deinosuchus, much like how the Leviathan is described, this prehistoric creature seems to have ruled its watery realm with unmatched strength and size.

Prayer:

Dear God, thank You for the mysteries of Your creation that humble us and remind us of Your power and presence. Help us to face our fears knowing You are with us, no matter what comes our way. Amen.

Creative Corner

DRAW A

LEVIATHAN

Or

Write a Short Story

READ THE AMAZING ADVENTURE OF JOB 41!
THEN, CREATE YOUR OWN INTERPRETATION OF THE MIGHTY
LEVIATHAN BASED ON THE VIVID DESCRIPTIONS IN THE
CHAPTER. DRAW THIS LEGENDARY CREATURE OR WRITE A
THRILLING SHORT STORY FEATURING ITS EPIC PRESENCE.
IMAGINE ITS SCALES, ITS POWER, AND THE AWE IT INSPIRES
AS DESCRIBED IN JOB. LET YOUR UNDERSTANDING OF THE
LEVIATHAN COME TO LIFE ON PAPER!

Day 2

The Strength of Behemoth

Scripture Spotlight:

"SEE NOW BEHEMOTH, WHICH I MADE AS WELL AS YOU. HE EATS GRASS AS AN OX. LOOK NOW, HIS STRENGTH IS IN HIS THIGHS. HIS FORCE IS IN THE MUSCLES OF HIS BELLY." JOB 40:15-16

Welcome Back and Get Ready to Trudge Through the Marsh:

Welcome to Day 2 of our biblical journey! Today, we trudge right into the marshlands to witness the awesome strength of the behemoth. As we read through Job 40, we encounter a mighty creature, a creature that can't be captured or tamed, and is unmatched in strength. It has limbs like beams of iron, a tail that sways like a cedar tree, and it makes the Earth tremble under its weight.

It eats grass like an ox, lives in the marshes under the Lotus plants, and even if there is a raging river, it is not disturbed. This marvel of God's creation is the Behemoth!

A Creature of Many Faces:

Similar to the leviathan, the Behemoth— or a creature with similar characteristics— can be found in tales from cultures around the globe. Some people envision this creature as a giant ox, an elephant, a hippopotamus, or a massive sauropod dinosaur that shook the ground with every step. Some people think the behemoth is a mythological symbol or idea. And then there are those who think the Behemoth is both a literal giant of the animal kingdom and a metaphor for the untamable aspects of creation.

A Glimpse of God's Power:

Whether the behemoth is a real-life creature or a symbolic one, the underlying lessons remain the same. In Job 40, we see that God used the behemoth to teach Job an important lesson of humility and help him see a bigger perspective. Job quickly realized that a powerful creature that commands respect and awe by all still remains under the control of its Creator. It reminds us that no matter how wild something may seem, everything is perfectly placed within God's grand design.

Today's Exploration:

As we read about the mighty behemoth and reflect on the wonders of God's creation, we can see that this incredible creature points us to a Creator who is powerful, wise, and in control. His creative power and plans are far beyond our understanding, and this challenges us to trust in God's strength and sovereignty, even when faced with the colossal challenges of our lives.

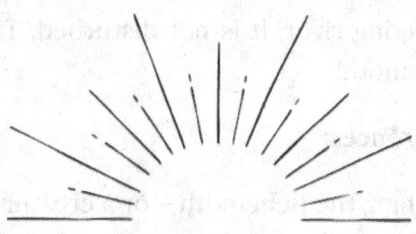

Let's Chat:

- How does reflecting on the power and majesty of creatures like the behemoth help us understand God's role as Creator and our place within His creation?

- How can we apply the lessons of humility and trust learned from the behemoth to our own lives, especially when faced with challenges beyond our control?

Prayer

Dear God, as we explore the mysteries of Your creation, please open our hearts and minds to the lessons that You want to teach us. Please help us to see Your power, wisdom, and care in all things, in Jesus' name, Amen.

Fun Fact: Ancient Artwork and Dinosaur Tales!

Did you know that ancient civilizations from all over the world have left behind captivating artwork featuring creatures that strikingly resemble dinosaurs? From intricate petroglyphs crafted by Native Americans to majestic Chinese sculptures, and even remarkable architectural designs from the Middle East, dinosaurs seem to have left their mark on human history. Ancient Greek pottery, Egyptian artifacts, and many other artifacts depict these awe-inspiring creatures, often depicted alongside known animals or even engaged in epic battles. It's like discovering a hidden world of ancient giants right alongside our own human history!

Creative Corner

READY FOR A PUZZLE CHALLENGE?

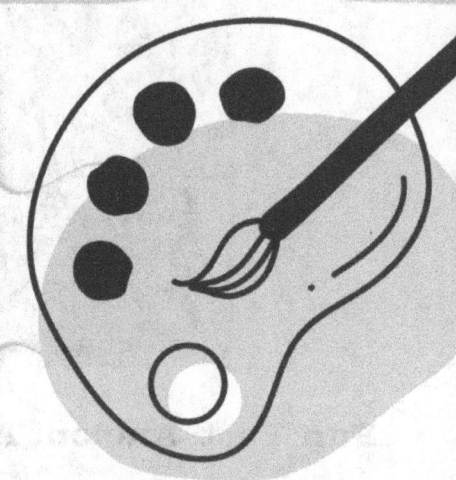

GRAB SOME MATERIALS LIKE A THIN CARDBOARD (THINK PIZZA OR CRACKER BOXES), OR THICK CONSTRUCTION PAPER.

THEN, LET YOUR IMAGINATION RUN WILD AS YOU COLOR OR PAINT A MAGNIFICENT SCENE FEATURING THE MIGHTY BEHEMOTH.

ONCE YOUR MASTERPIECE IS COMPLETE, IT'S TIME TO MAKE SOME PUZZLE PIECES! GRAB A PENCIL AND CAREFULLY DESIGN YOUR PIECES THEN CUT THEM OUT WITH A SHARP SCISSOR.

FINALLY, PASS YOUR PUZZLE CREATION TO ANOTHER FAMILY MEMBER!

Day 3

Skipping Along Like a Unicorn

Scripture Spotlight:

"HE MAKES THEM ALSO TO SKIP LIKE A CALF; LEBANON AND SIRION LIKE A YOUNG, WILD OX." PSALMS 29:6

Unicorn Quest: A Biblical Adventure

Welcome back to Day 3 of our thrilling journey through *Amazing Biblical Creatures*! Today, we're skipping over to the enchanting land of unicorns. Yes, you heard that right! Did you know that unicorns are mentioned in the Bible? That's right—these mystical creatures aren't just for fairy tales! Let's flip through the pages of the King James Version (KJV) of the Bible and set off on a thrilling unicorn scavenger hunt. Your quest is to discover the unicorns hidden within these scriptures:

- Numbers 23:22

- Numbers 24:8

- Deuteronomy 33:17

- Job 39:9

- Job 39:10

- Psalm 22:21

- Psalm 29:6

- Psalm 92:10

- Isaiah 34:7

The Real Unicorns of the Bible

As you explore these verses, you'll quickly realize that the Bible's unicorns are not the glittering, rainbow-maned stallions of modern imagination. Instead, they are described as powerful creatures, symbolizing strength and majesty. The term "unicorn" in the 1828 Webster's Dictionary is defined as "an animal with one horn; the monoceros," often thought to be a rhinoceros. Meanwhile, other translations refer to the original Hebrew word 're'em' as a wild ox.

A Tale of Translation and Truth

Why does the KJV use "unicorn"? Some scholars argue it was a mistranslation, while others believe it was the most accurate term available at the time to describe a one-horned animal. This linguistic puzzle does not diminish the Bible's accuracy or truthfulness. Despite variations in word choice, the essence of the Bible remains unchanged across translations and centuries. Scholarly comparisons of ancient texts, like the Masoretic Text, the Septuagint, and the Dead Sea Scrolls, reveal a remarkable consistency in the Bible's message.

Let's Chat:

- How do you feel when you hear that the Bible mentions unicorns?

- If someone says the Bible isn't true because it talks about unicorns, what could you say?

Prayer:

Dear Father, as we reflect on today's journey, we are grateful for the profound richness of the Bible and the captivating world it unveils. Grant us the wisdom to comprehend Your Words as You intend, and empower us to apply Your truths in our daily lives. In Jesus' name, we pray. Amen.

Fun Fact: The Unicorn: Fact or Fantasy?

Here's a fun fact to spark your imagination: scientists have discovered fossils of a creature called Elasmotherium sibiricum, also known as the Siberian unicorn. This giant beast, believed to have a single large horn, stood about 2 meters tall and stretched 4.5 meters long!

Creative Corner

A Biblical Scavenger Hunt!

1

Craft Your Clues: Everyone in the family picks a scripture verse from the Bible. It could be anything from the strength of a unicorn to the wisdom of Solomon. Write down your verse on a piece of paper.

2

Hide your scripture somewhere around the house. Now, the creative part—write a riddle that hints at where your verse is hidden. For example, "Your adventure begins where words of life abundantly abound. Find me where morning light is first found." This riddle could lead your family members to a sunny spot by a window where the first rays of the sun touch your home.

3

Exchange your riddle with another family member. Each person gets a turn to solve a riddle and find the hidden scripture. It's like a treasure hunt but with the added joy of discovering God's Word!

Double the Fun:

Want to make it even more thrilling? Add a second part to your riddle that leads to a small prize or a fun activity related to the verse.

Day 4

Fee Fi Fo Fum, Here the Giants Come!

Scripture spotlight:

"(FOR ONLY OG KING OF BASHAN REMAINED OF THE REMNANT OF THE REPHAIM. BEHOLD, HIS BEDSTEAD WAS A BEDSTEAD OF IRON. ISN'T IT IN RABBAH OF THE CHILDREN OF AMMON? NINE CUBITS WAS ITS LENGTH, AND FOUR CUBITS ITS WIDTH, AFTER THE CUBIT OF A MAN.)" - DEUTERONOMY 3:11

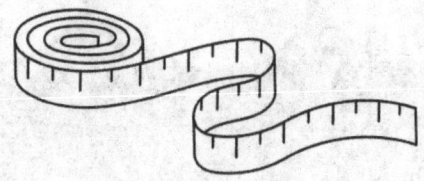

Gigantic Beginnings: The Tale of King Og

Welcome back to another exciting day of *Amazing Biblical Creatures!* Today, we step into the enormous shoes of King Og of Bashan, one of the last giants known as the Rephaim. Imagine the bed mentioned in this scripture—not just large, but colossal, measuring about 13.5 feet by 6 feet! This artifact, a testament to his giant stature, challenges us to envision a world where such immense beings lived among humans.

Courageous Leadership: Joshua's Challenge

In the book of Joshua, we learn that Joshua was chosen to lead the Israelites into the Promised Land, a land flowing with milk and honey but also inhabited by giants and formidable enemies. As Joshua prepared to lead his people into unknown lands, the Lord provided encouragement and strength. Joshua 1:9 resonates with divine assurance, "Have I not commanded you? Be strong and courageous. Do not be frightened, and do not be dismayed, for the Lord your God is with you wherever you go." This powerful message reminds us that with faith, we can face any challenge, no matter how daunting.

Facing Goliath: David's Victory

The story of young David facing the Philistine giant, Goliath, in 1 Samuel 17, is not just an underdog tale but a profound lesson in faith. Armed with only a sling and a few stones, David confronted Goliath, who boasted massive armor and weapons. Against all odds, David proclaimed, "The battle is the Lord's," showcasing his unwavering faith in God's supremacy over any physical threat.

1. <u>Prayer:</u> Just as David prayed before his battle with Goliath, we, too, can seek strength and guidance through prayer when facing our giants.

2. <u>Faith:</u> Remember, God is always with us, just as He was with Joshua, leading the Israelites into a land of giants. Our faith can move mountains and defeat giants.

3. <u>Courage:</u> Facing our fears is the first step toward victory. Courage means acting despite fear, knowing that God's strength is made perfect in our weakness.

Let's Chat:

- Imagine you are an archaeologist who discovers the remains of a giant's bed. What else would you like to find to tell you more about their life?

- How does the Bible teach us to respond to the giants we encounter?

Prayer:

Dear God, please infuse us with the courage and faith we need to face our giant obstacles. May we draw inspiration and encouragement from the stories of David, Joshua, and King Og. Please help us to remember that with You, no challenge or obstacle is too big. In Jesus' name, Amen.

Fun fact: Giant Discoveries

Imagine walking through your garden and stumbling upon a hidden treasure... Well, that's exactly what happened in the spring of 1962! An Israeli farmer was just plowing his field in Kfar Monash when he hit something unbelievable - a stash of ancient goodies hidden beneath the soil.

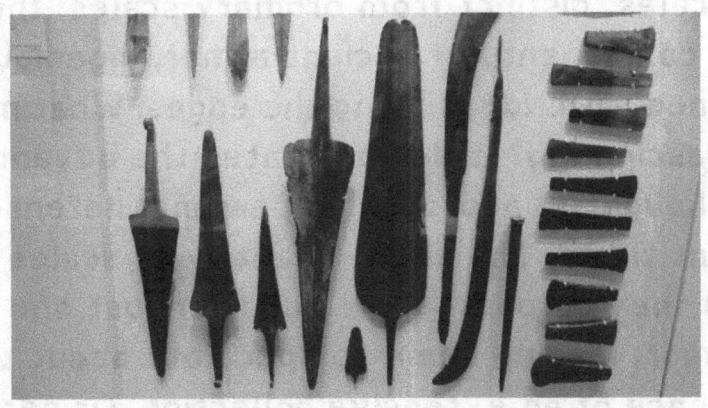

Spearheads Like No Other: Among these incredible finds were some massive copper spearheads. Picture this: one of them was 66cm (over 2 feet) long! That's huge, especially when you think that most spearheads from back then were just about 6cm. It's like comparing a pencil to a yardstick.

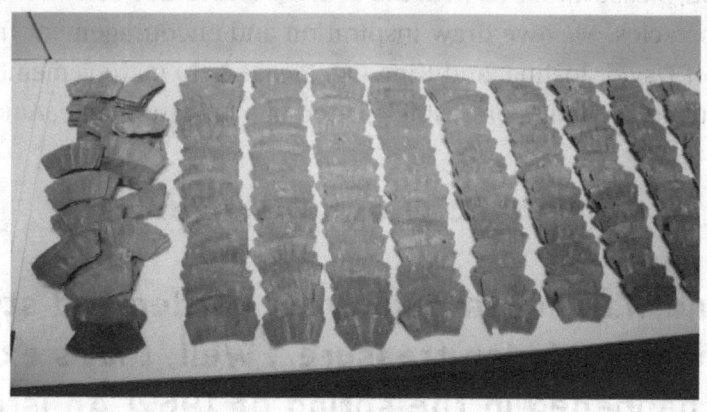

Armor Galore: But there's even more to this tale! The farmer unearthed approximately 800 copper scales, distinct from ordinary scales; these were components of ancient armor, ingeniously designed with ridges along the edges. What makes this fascinating? It demonstrates the advanced and thoughtful approach to personal defense in ancient times. The sheer quantity of scales suggests they surpassed the need for just one suit of armor, leading some to speculate about the existence of an extensive collection. Or perhaps, could these scales have been part of a singular, exceptionally large piece of armor?

Creative Corner

GIANT MAP

CREATE A "GIANT MAP."
THIS MAP WON'T FEATURE LITERAL GIANTS, BUT INSTEAD, IT WILL SHOWCASE THE CHALLENGES EACH FAMILY MEMBER IS FACING. DRAW OR LIST THESE CHALLENGES ON THE MAP. THEN, TOGETHER, BRAINSTORM WAYS TO CONQUER THESE CHALLENGES THROUGH FAITH, PRAYER, AND COURAGE. THIS ACTIVITY WILL REMIND YOU THAT NO CHALLENGE IS TOO GREAT FOR GOD. AS A FAMILY UNITED IN FAITH,
YOU CAN OVERCOME ANYTHING!

KING OG'S BED

Ever wondered how big King Og's bed was? Grab a tape measure and some masking tape, or head outside with some chalk. Measure and tape off (or draw with chalk) a rectangle on the ground that's 13.5 feet in length and 6 feet in width.

This hands-on activity will help you visualize the immense size of these biblical giants and imagine the world in which they lived. It's a fun and engaging way to bring the Bible to life!

Day 5

Heavenly Worshipers

Scripture spotlight:

"Then one of the seraphim flew to me, having a live coal in his hand, which he had taken with the tongs from off the altar. He touched my mouth with it, and said, 'Behold, this has touched your lips; and your iniquity is taken away, and your sin forgiven.'" - Isaiah 6:6-7

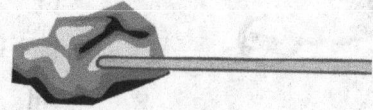

Encountering the Seraphim

Welcome to Day 5 of our extraordinary journey through the Bible's most awe-inspiring creatures! Today, we're soaring into the celestial realms to stand among the seraphim—divine beings who radiate with the glory of God Himself. Immortalized in Isaiah 6:1-7, these beings captivate us with their six-winged splendor: two wings shield their faces in awe of God, two cover their feet in humility, and two carry them as they soar through the heavens.

The Meaning Behind the Flames

Dr. Michael Heiser, a renowned biblical scholar, unveils that "seraphim" stems from "saraph," a word that intriguingly means both "serpent" and "to burn." Thus, "Seraphim" could translate to "the burning ones," a title that mirrors their fiery essence and their role as both guardians and worshipers at God's throne. Their fiery nature may not only define their appearance but also illuminate their divine purpose: to purify, to reveal God's holiness, and to serve as celestial proclaimers of His glory.

When the prophet Isaiah stands amidst these divine creatures, he's overwhelmed by a sense of unworthiness. In a symbolic act of cleansing, one seraph purifies Isaiah's lips with burning coal, preparing him to speak God's truths. This timeless moment teaches us about the transformative power of God's presence and the seraphim's sacred role in sanctifying those who are called to serve.

Echoing Celestial Praise

The seraphim's ceaseless proclamation, "Holy, holy, holy, is Yahweh of Armies! The whole earth is full of his glory!" is a powerful reminder of the depth of worship. Their existence is a testament to the majesty and sanctity of God, inviting us to reflect on the heart of true worship: recognizing God's unparalleled holiness and finding joy in His presence.

Let's Chat:

- What can we learn from the way the seraphim serve God?

- In what ways can we, as families, acknowledge and honor God's holiness in our daily lives?

Prayer:

Dear Lord, teach us to worship You with the purity and passion of the seraphim. Please help us reflect Your holiness in our lives and learn how to continuously sing Your praises. May Your glory fill our hearts and guide our actions. In Jesus' name, Amen.

Fun Fact: Winged Snakes of the Ancient World

 Did you know that ancient texts and artifacts are filled with tales of mysterious winged creatures? The renowned Greek historian Herodotus, writing around 460 BC, shared stories of winged snakes. These tales, originating from Arabian sources, described the flying serpents that dwelled near the frankincense trees of the Arabian Desert. To harvest the precious resin, the Arabians would use smoke to repel these snakes. The winged snakes were depicted as small, with vibrant markings and bat-like wings. While modern science has yet to uncover evidence of their existence, Herodotus's accounts remain a captivating part of ancient lore. Additionally, the frequent depiction of flying snakes in Egyptian art, on clothing, and in statues highlights their symbolic importance in ancient cultures

Creative Corner

IGNITE YOUR FAITH

GATHER YOUR FAMILY FOR AN EXCITING CAMPFIRE NIGHT THAT BRINGS THE BIBLE TO LIFE!

JUST LIKE THE SERAPHIM USED A FIERY COAL TO PURIFY ISAIAH, YOU CAN USE MARSHMALLOWS TO SYMBOLIZE THIS SPECIAL MOMENT.

AS YOU ROAST MARSHMALLOWS ON STICKS, IMAGINE THEY ARE THE PURIFYING COAL, SHARING WARMTH AND LIGHT.

TAKE TURNS SHARING YOUR PERSONAL CHALLENGES OR MISSTEPS AND REFLECT ON HOW JESUS' SACRIFICE PURIFIES US.

THIS FUN AND MEANINGFUL ACTIVITY WILL REMIND YOU OF GOD'S ENDLESS CAPACITY TO CLEANSE AND RENEW.

No Marshmallows?

Sing Praises!

No marshmallows, no problem!
Turn your home into a joyful concert
by gathering your family to sing praises to our
"Holy, Holy, Holy" God.
Lift your voices in worship and fill your home
with the sound of adoration and gratitude.
This lively and heartwarming activity will help
everyone feel connected to God through music and
togetherness.

Day 6

Balaam's Donkey - A Lesson in Listening

Scripture Spotlight

"Yahweh opened the mouth of the donkey, and she said to Balaam, 'What have I done to you, that you have struck me these three times?'" - Numbers 22:28

A Tale of Divine Intervention

Welcome to Day 6 of our journey through *Amazing Biblical Creatures*! Today, we explore a story where God's wisdom is revealed through an unexpected source: Balaam's donkey. This narrative highlights a miraculous event and teaches us valuable lessons about obedience, the dangers of greed, and the reliability of God's protective promises.

Balaam's Temptation and Divine Guidance

Imagine being offered a treasure chest full of gold to do something you know is wrong. That's precisely what happened to Balaam. King Balak promised him riches to curse the Israelites. Despite knowing it went against God's will, Balaam was tempted. Initially refusing, he eventually set off, perhaps believing he could find a loophole in God's instructions. But God had other plans. An angel of the Lord stood in Balaam's path, invisible to him but visible to his donkey. Frustrated, Balaam beat the donkey until God miraculously gave the animal the ability to speak. Imagine the surprise when, after beating the donkey, Balaam hears the animal speak! This extraordinary event opened Balaam's eyes to the angel standing before him, a powerful reminder that God's plans cannot be outwitted.

A Lesson in Divine Protection

This story illustrates that God's blessings cannot be overturned by human intentions. It serves as a reminder that when God says "no," He means it. Attempting to twist His words or act against His will only leads us astray. It's a lesson about wholeheartedly listening to God and trusting in His protective promises.

Let's Chat:

- How does Balaam's story emphasize the importance of listening to God?

- Have you ever tried to turn a "no" into a "yes," or sought a loophole in the rules? What was the outcome?

Prayer:

Heavenly Father, thank You for the lessons from Balaam and his donkey. Please help us listen to Your guidance, choose obedience over temptation, and trust in Your protective care. May we learn to hear and follow Your voice, even when the path seems difficult or unclear. In Jesus' name, Amen.

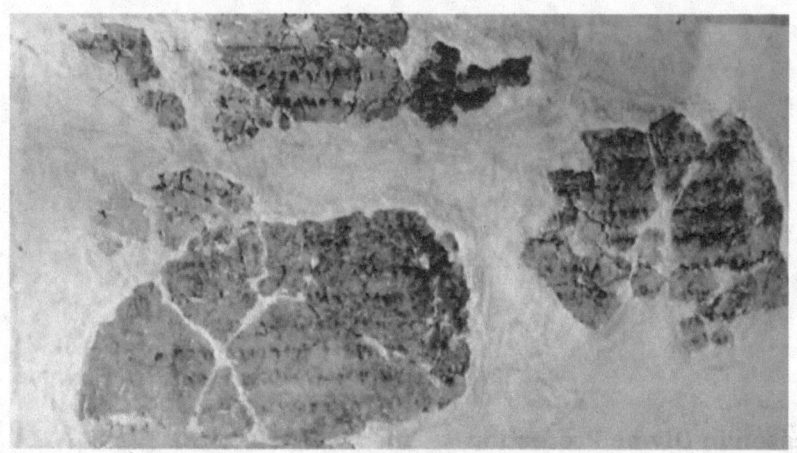

Fun Fact: Unearthing Balaam's Legacy

Did you know an ancient inscription mentioning Balaam, the biblical prophet, was uncovered by archaeologists? On March 17, 1967, a groundbreaking discovery was made at Tell Deir Alla in the Jordan Valley by Jordanian excavator Ali Abdul-Rasul. He found traces of letters on tiny plaster pieces, revealing what is now known as the Deir Alla Inscription. These fragments, dating back to the late 9th or early 8th century BCE, narrate a vision received by Balaam, warning of impending disaster. This significant find highlights Balaam's importance across various cultures of his time, illustrating the widespread recognition of his prophetic role.

Creative Corner
NAVIGATING MAZES

Get ready for a thrilling hands-on activity that reflects the twists and turns of life's choices, inspired by the story of Balaam!

Here's How:

Each family member will design a unique maze on paper. But these aren't just ordinary mazes; they should include tempting routes that seem appealing but lead to dead ends, symbolizing life's misleading options.

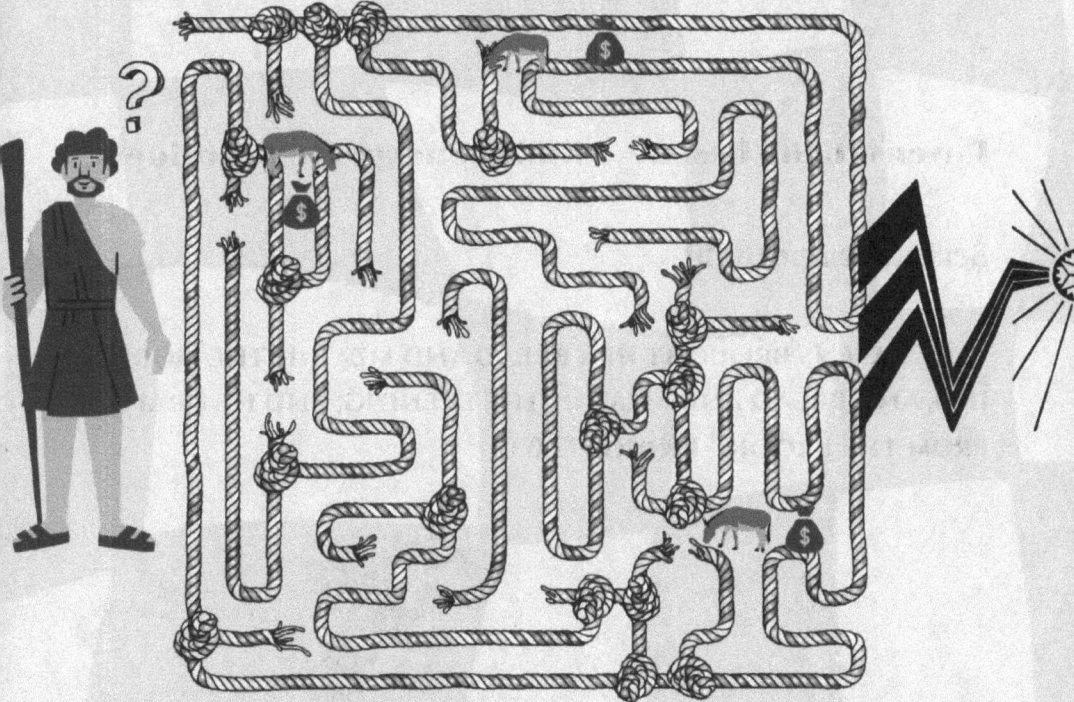

Once everyone has crafted their mazes, the fun begins! Exchange your mazes and challenge each other to navigate through them. As you work through the paths, notice how, just like in the mazes, we may encounter enticing but misleading paths in life. Talk about how recognizing and resisting these paths with faith can help us find our way to the right path.

Day 7

Ravens to the Rescue - Elijah's Unexpected Providers

Scripture Spotlight

"THE RAVENS BROUGHT HIM BREAD AND MEAT IN THE MORNING, AND BREAD AND MEAT IN THE EVENING; AND HE DRANK FROM THE BROOK." 1 KINGS 17:6

Feathered Providers in a Time of Need

Welcome to the final day of our exploration of the Bible's most amazing creatures! Today, we marvel at the miraculous story of the ravens who fed Prophet Elijah. During a severe drought, these unlikely heroes were God's chosen messengers, bringing sustenance to Elijah and demonstrating God's ability to provide in the most unexpected ways.

Elijah's Leap of Faith

Imagine the prophet Elijah, living in a time when the skies had closed up, no rain in sight, following God's command to retreat to the Brook Cherith. Picture him thirsty and alone by the brook, when suddenly, he sees a raven soaring in with food in its beak—a delivery straight from God. There, God promises an extraordinary delivery service: ravens, birds not typically known for their sharing nature, bringing bread 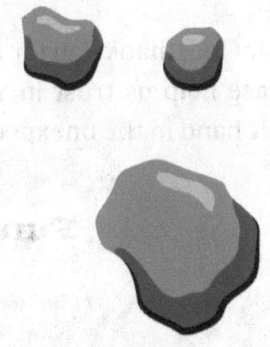 and meat morning and evening. This divine arrangement not only sustained Elijah but also reinforced the lesson that God's ways are boundless and often come through surprising means.

The Message of the Ravens

These remarkable ravens, heeding God's call, remind us that the Lord can use all of creation to meet our needs, particularly during tough times. This story encourages us to place our trust in God's care and stay open to the miraculous ways He might intervene in our lives. Echoing Jesus' assurance, "Consider the ravens: they don't sow, they don't reap, they have no warehouse or barn, and God feeds them. How much more valuable are you than birds!" - Luke 12:24, we're reminded of our worth and God's care for us.

Let's Chat:

- How does the story of Elijah and the ravens inspire us to trust in God's plans?

- Can you recall a time when help came to you in an unexpected way?

Prayer:

Dear God, thank You for reminding us of Your endless provision and care. Please help us trust in You wholeheartedly, and teach us to recognize Your hand in the unexpected blessings of our lives. In Jesus' name, Amen.

Fun Fact: Brainy Birds

Ever thought birds could converse or even clean up parks? Ravens and crows shatter all expectations! These feathered wonders are not just brainy; they're downright brilliant. Ravens have been observed mimicking human speech with astonishing accuracy, sometimes even better than parrots. But that's not all—these clever birds have been trained in places like Sweden and France to collect trash in exchange for food rewards. Special devices dispense treats when they deposit litter, making them eco-warriors in the fight against pollution!

Creative Corner

"RAVENS' TREASURE HUNT"

Discover how teamwork can triumph over individual effort, just like the ravens that provided for Elijah!

Materials Needed:

- Various small items (coins, toys, or colored stones)
- Timer (smartphone or stopwatch)
- Basket or container for collected items

Preparation:

- Choose one family member to play Elijah.
- Elijah hides or scatters the items around your home or yard. (Tip: Take notes of where you hid them!)

HOW TO PLAY:

Solo Round:

- Time each family member as they search individually for the items and bring them to Elijah within 1-3 minutes.
- Note their times and how many items they find.

Team Round:

- Re-hide the items.
- Work together as a team of "ravens" to find and bring the items to Elijah within the same time frame.
- Compare the results of the solo and team rounds.

DID YOU NOTICE HOW TEAMWORK NOT ONLY SPED UP THE PROCESS BUT ALSO MADE IT MORE FUN?
THIS GAME ISN'T MERELY ABOUT FINDING HIDDEN TREASURES;
IT BRINGS THE STORY OF ELIJAH TO LIFE,
DEMONSTRATING THE POWER OF UNITY AND COOPERATION.

CHAPTER 3
WEAPONS OF THE BIBLE
Getting Our Hands on a Few Fascinating Weapons

"THE ARROW OF DELIVERANCE"
DALZIEL BROTHERS

Day 1

The Jawbone of a Donkey

Scripture Spotlight

"He found a fresh jawbone of a donkey, put out his hand, took it, and struck a thousand men with it." - Judges 15:15

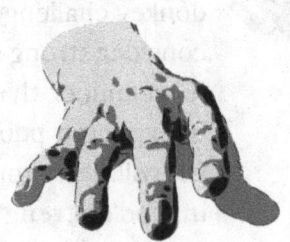

Unlikely Tools for Mighty Deeds

Welcome to the thrilling start of our journey through the *Weapons of the Bible*. Today, we are cast into the extraordinary
tale of Samson and his unconventional
weapon of choice: the jawbone of a donkey. Among his many feats, this moment
stands as a testament to God's power to
empower and deliver through the most
unexpected means.

Samson: The Unstoppable Force

Chosen by God to deliver Israel from the Philistines, Samson sought
to right the wrongs against his people. Cornered by his enemies and
without a conventional weapon, he grabbed what was at hand—a fresh
jawbone of a donkey. With it, he secured a staggering victory, defeating
a thousand men. This incredible act shows that God can use anyone and
anything to help us overcome overwhelming odds, demonstrating that
divine purposes can be fulfilled with whatever is at hand, no matter how
unconventional.

Lessons from the Jawbone

Samson's victory with the jawbone of a
donkey challenges us to rethink what we
consider strong and useful. It's a powerful reminder that God can use the most
unexpected people and things to fulfill
His will. This story encourages us to trust
in God's strength and be open to how
He might work through us in surprising
ways.

Let's Chat:

- How does Samson's use of the jawbone inspire us to view our challenges?

- Can you think of a moment when you felt empowered to accomplish something difficult?

Prayer:

Heavenly Father, thank You for the lesson of Samson and the jawbone, which teaches us that You can use anything to fulfill Your purposes. Please help us see the potential in what we have and trust in Your strength, especially when we feel powerless. May we be reminded of Your creativity and sovereignty in all circumstances. In Jesus' name, Amen.

Fun Fact: The Mystical Sounds of the Donkey Jawbone Rattle

Ever imagined a musical instrument crafted from a donkey jawbone?

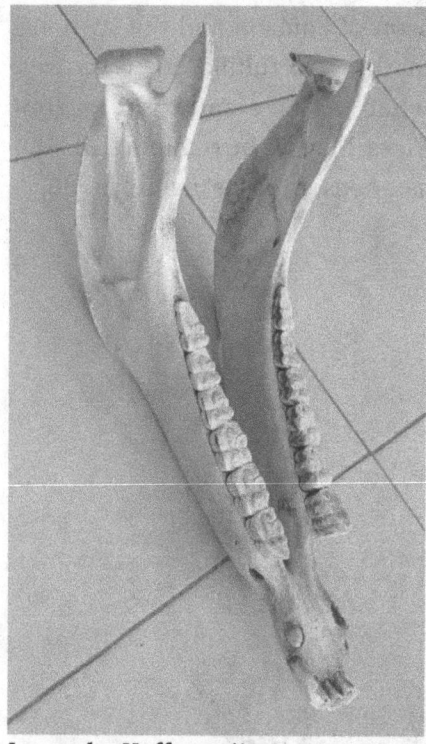

Image by Koffermejia

Yes, you heard that right! Welcome to the world of the "Quijada," a natural rattle instrument that transforms a donkey's jawbone into a symphony of unique sounds. Picture this: a musician taps the side of the jawbone, and as if by magic, the teeth inside come alive, dancing and rattling to create mesmerizing music. Intrigued? Dive into the rabbit hole of YouTube, where you can witness the Quijada in action, revealing its distinctive and fascinating sounds.

Creative Corner

SAMSON'S RETURN CHALLENGE

LET'S CRAFT A BOOMERANG!

Although the Bible doesn't mention Samson wielding the jawbone of a donkey like a boomerang, its shape gives us a fun way to explore themes of return, effort, and the unexpected in Samson's story.

GET READY FOR THE CHALLENGE!

Crafting a boomerang from household supplies isn't just a fun activity—it's also a chance to talk about resilience and divine intervention, just like in Samson's adventures. While our boomerangs might not fly perfectly, the fun and learning along the way are what count!

Materials Needed:

- Cardboard
- Pencil
- Scissors
- Ruler
- Markers or paint

INSTRUCTIONS

1. **Design Your Boomerang:**
   - Draw a boomerang shape on your cardboard, making a wide 'V' with slightly curved arms.
   - Each arm should be about 8-12 inches long and 2 inches wide.

2. **Cut Out the Boomerang:**
   - Carefully cut along your design with scissors.
   - For a sturdier boomerang, cut multiple pieces and glue them together.

3. **Decorate:**
   - Use markers or paint to decorate your boomerang. Add patterns, messages, or even design it to look like a jawbone.

4. **Fold the Arms:**
   - Twist the ends of each arm upwards (one arm in the opposite direction of the other) to create a slight 'S' curve. This helps your boomerang fly better.

5. **Test and Tweak:**
   - In an open area, gently toss your boomerang.
   - Experiment with different twists and angles to improve its flight. Getting it to return is tricky, but that's part of the fun!

Enjoy the challenge and remember, just like Samson, persistence and effort can lead to amazing results!

Day 2

David's Sling and Stone

Scripture Spotlight

"Then David said to the Philistine, 'You come to me with a sword, with a spear, and with a javelin; but I come to you in the name of Yahweh of Armies, the God of the armies of Israel, whom you have defied.'" - 1 Samuel 17:45

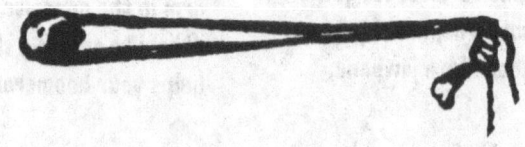

David's Unwavering Faith

On Day 2 of our journey through the *Weapons of the Bible*, we encounter the young shepherd David, standing boldly before the giant Goliath. In this pivotal moment, David's words echo through time, a declaration of his unwavering faith in the Lord. His confidence wasn't rooted in physical weaponry or brute strength but in the might of Yahweh of Armies, the true God of Israel.

Setting the Scene

Imagine the scene: The Israelites were facing off against the Philistines, a fearsome enemy known for their powerful warriors and advanced weaponry. The Philistines had dominated the region, and their greatest warrior, Goliath, was an intimidating giant who struck fear into the hearts of all who saw him. The Israelites, on the other hand, were mostly shepherds and farmers, seemingly no match for such a powerful foe. Yet, in this tense standoff, young David stepped forward—not as a soldier, but as a simple shepherd boy with unshakable faith. With nothing but a sling, a few stones, and his trust in God, David was ready to face the giant who had terrorized his people.

The Power Behind the Stone

David's choice to face Goliath with just a sling and a stone wasn't a sign of his limitations; it was a profound demonstration of his faith. He knew that victory was already his—not because of what he held in his hand, but because of Who he held in his heart. This act serves as a timeless reminder that with God, all things are possible and that our greatest battles are won through faith, not force

Let's Chat:

- How does David's confidence in the Lord inspire you to approach your challenges with faith?

- Have you ever experienced a time when your faith gave you the courage to face a tough situation?

Prayer:

Heavenly Father, thank You for the inspiring story of David and his victory over Goliath. Please help us to remember that, like David, our strength and victory come from You. May we face our most challenging situations with faith like David, knowing that You are with us, ready to step forward when You need us to. In Jesus' name, Amen.

Fun Fact: A Sling's Precision

Did you know? David's sling wasn't just a simple child's toy—it was a powerful ancient weapon known as a Balearic sling, renowned for its incredible precision!

Unlike the modern Y-shaped sling-shots you might be thinking of, David's Balearic sling was a simple but highly effective tool made of a long piece of leather or fabric with  a pouch in the middle. Skilled slingers would place a stone in the pouch, swing it rapidly above their heads, and then release one end of the sling to launch the stone at incredible speeds. Imagine this: Skilled slingers could hurl stones with such speed and accuracy that they could hit targets over 200 meters (660 feet) away! The force of a stone launched from a Balearic sling could be as deadly as a bullet fired from a handgun, capable of striking with enough power to seriously injure or even take down a warrior in full armor. So when David stepped onto that battlefield, he wasn't just armed with a sling—he was wielding a weapon that, in the hands of someone with faith and skill, could deliver a knockout blow to any giant!

Creative Corner

DAVID'S SLING

(BALEARIC SLING)

Get ready to step back in time and experience history firsthand!
Crafting your very own sling brings the epic story of David and Goliath to life, while showing the incredible skills ancient shepherds needed for herding and protection. Just like David, you'll discover that mastering the sling takes practice and perfect timing, reminding us of the importance of patience and faith in our spiritual journey.

MATERIALS:

- One piece of leather or durable fabric (approx. 2 inches wide and 8 inches long for the pouch and connecting cords)
- Two lengths of string, rope, or paracord (each about 30 inches long, but you can adjust based on the user's arm length and comfort)
- Scissors

USING YOUR SLING:

1. Practice Grip: Place the loop of the retention cord around your finger (usually the index or middle finger), and hold the release cord between your thumb and forefinger.
2. Load Your Sling: Place a small ball in the pouch's center.
3. Swing and Release: Swing the sling overhead or beside you to build momentum. To release the ball, simply let go of the release cord at the right moment to aim your shot. Note: Start with gentle swings and practice in an open, safe area away from people and breakables.

INSTRUCTIONS:

1. Cut the Pouch: Cut your leather or fabric into a 2-inch by 8-inch rectangle. This will be the pouch for holding the stone.
2. Attach the Cords: Punch or cut small holes at each corner of the pouch.
- Thread a string through each hole on one short side, securing with a knot. Repeat on the other side. These strings are your release and retention cords.
3. Prepare the Cords:
- On the retention cord (the one you'll hold), tie a loop large enough for your middle finger.
- The release cord (the one you'll let go of) can be left as is, or tie a small knot at the end for easier grip and identification.

SAFETY AND TIPS:

- This should be done with adult supervision.
- Practice in an open area where there's no risk of accidentally hitting someone or something fragile.
- Begin with soft, lightweight objects like foam balls to learn the motion.

Day 3

The Sword of Victory

Scripture Spotlight

"Joshua defeated Amalek and his people with the edge of the sword." - Exodus 17:13

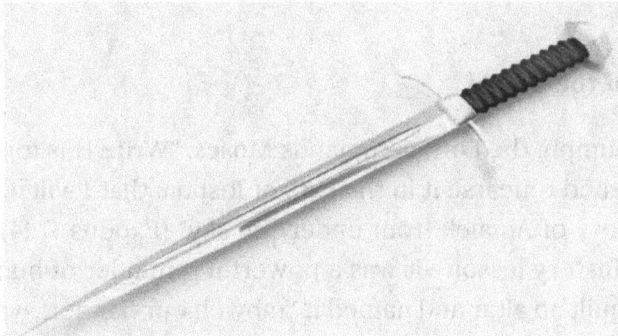

The Clash at Rephidim

Grab your helmet and get ready as we charge into Day 3 of our journey through *Weapons of the Bible*. Today, our focus sharpens on the sword—a symbol recognized across ages for its authority and justice. But in the heart-pounding battle at Rephidim, we discover that true authority and justice come from God Himself, as His power flows through this weapon in Joshua's hands. As Joshua bravely leads others in the battle, his sword transcends mere metal; it becomes a vessel of divine verdict, delivering a resounding victory for God's people.

The Sword and Strategy

The battle at Rephidim was no ordinary skir-mish—it was a clash of faith, strategy, and obe-dience. Joshua, armed with his sword, con-fronts the battlefield head-on, while Moses, Aaron, and Hur offer their support from a hilltop. Impressively, when Moses raises his hands, Israel gains the upper hand. But endurance has its limits. As fatigue set in and Moses' arms grew tired, Aaron and Hur  stepped up, holding his arms steady until sunset. This powerful act of teamwork and faith was a clear sign to everyone that true victory comes not from human strength alone but from unwavering trust in God's might.

The Lesson of the Sword

After their triumph, the Lord commands Moses, "Write this for a memo-rial in a book, and rehearse it in the ears of Joshua: that I will utterly blot out the memory of Amalek from under the sky" (Exodus 17:14). But this wasn't just a history lesson—it was a powerful reminder of humility and faith. Moses built an altar and named it 'Yahweh our Banner,' symbolizing that God is the one who leads us to victory. Like Joshua, we are called to face our challenges with bravery, armed not by our own strength, but bolstered by our steadfast faith in the Almighty.

Let's Chat:

- How can Joshua's epic victory at Rephidim inspire us to face our own battles with faith?

- Why do you think God wanted this story written down to be remembered for generations?

Prayer:

Heavenly Father, as we reflect on the story of Joshua and the epic battle at Rephidim, we are reminded of Your unmatched power and the victory that comes from placing our trust in You. Thank You for the example of Moses, Aaron, and Hur—united together to support one another. Like Joshua, please help us have the courage to face our battles, knowing that You're the banner we look to and fight for. May we always lean on You and support others in their battles, too. In Jesus' name, we pray, Amen.

Fun Fact: Swords Through Time!

 Did you know the journey of the sword is said to have begun in the Middle East around 3000 BC? Back then, swords were a rare sight, crafted from the metals available at the time. It wasn't until the Middle Ages, with advancements in metallurgy, that swords became the iconic weapons we imagine—forged from stronger metals and designed for battle and ceremony alike. The sword's journey is as rich and varied as human history itself!

Creative Corner

VICTORY SWORD BOOKMARK

This isn't just any bookmark—it's your unique creation. Imagine wielding the sword of your dreams, complete with a verse that encourages you to be brave and have faith.

MATERIALS:

- A piece of cardstock or any thick paper
- Scissors
- Markers, crayons, paint, colored pencils or pens

INSTRUCTIONS:

SKETCH A SWORD:

On your cardstock, draw the most epic sword you can imagine. Use a ruler for straight lines on the blade. Make it about the length of your hand so it fits perfectly in your book!

CUT IT OUT:

Carefully cut along your drawing to bring your sword to life. Feel the excitement as your bookmark takes shape!

DECORATE THE BLADE:

Grab your markers, pens, or crayons and add some cool details to the blade. Draw lines to make it look shiny and sharp. Imagine you're a master sword-maker, designing a blade that can cut through any adventure!

DECORATE THE HANDLE:

Now for the fun part! Decorate the handle to make it stand out. Want to add some strings or ribbons? Go for it!

WRITE A FIGHTER VERSE:

On the blade, write a short, powerful quote from your devotional or your favorite Bible verse. Choose something that makes you feel strong and ready to take on the day!

BOOKMARK READY!

And just like that, you've forged your very own Victory Sword Bookmark. Use it to keep your place in your devotional or any book you're reading, and let it remind you of God's strength every day.

Day 4

Arrows of Faith

Scripture Spotlight

"AS ARROWS IN THE HAND OF A MIGHTY MAN, SO ARE THE
CHILDREN OF YOUTH." - PSALM 127:4

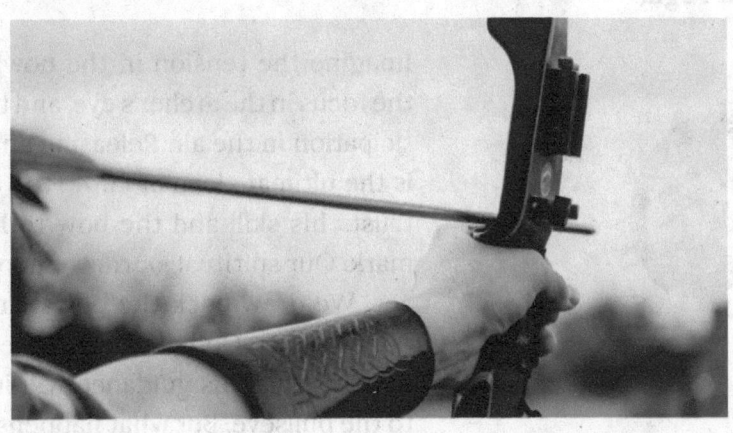

The Adventure of Arrows

Grab your quiver and get ready to begin Day 4 of our *Weapons of the Bible journey*, where we set our sights on the thrilling world of archery. Arrows aren't just tools of warfare; they're symbols packed with meaning—representing direction, protection, and the fulfillment of God's will. Imagine each arrow as a source of intention, soaring through the air with precision and purpose, guided by the hand of a skilled archer.

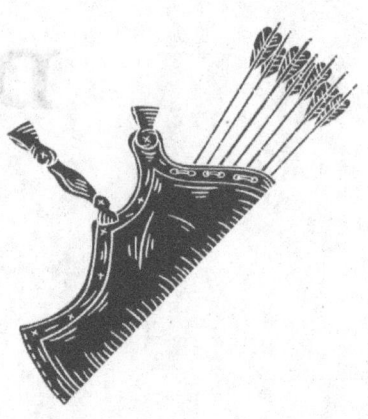

Archery: A Lesson in Life

Archery in biblical times, and even today, isn't just a skill—it's an art form demanding patience, focus, and practice. The Psalmist's comparison of children to arrows brings this art to life, illustrating the crucial role of careful guidance in shaping our paths and others' toward God's targets. Like an expert archer, we're invited to take aim with purpose, ensuring our life's trajectory aligns with our Father's intentions.

Faith in Flight

Imagine the tension in the bowstring, the focus in the archer's eye, and the anticipation in the air. Releasing an arrow is the ultimate leap of faith—the archer trusts his skill and the bow to hit the mark. Our spiritual journey mirrors this act. We draw back the bowstring, set our sights on God's target, and let it fly, trusting that His guidance will lead us to the bullseye. But what happens when we lose focus, get distracted, or miss the mark? It's important to remember that we all miss sometimes. When we do, we shouldn't give up or lose hope. Jesus took all the missed shots, corrected our wrongs, and continues to give us a brand new target to shoot at. If we are willing to listen and seek His guidance, He teaches us where we went wrong and what we can do to improve. Each arrow, each action propelled by faith, has the potential to strike true when we aim for God's glory. And remember, even when we miss, God's grace guides us back on course, helping us grow stronger with every shot.

Let's Chat:

- **Precision and Posture:** What steps must an archer take to ensure their arrow flies true? Think about their posture, focus, and attitude. How does this careful preparation mirror the way we should approach our own lives and challenges? How can we align our actions with God's purpose?

- **Life's Arrows:** Just as an archer aims their arrow with intention and skill, how can we similarly direct the 'arrows' in our lives—our actions, decisions, and words—toward meaningful and positive impacts?

Prayer:

Heavenly Father, thank You for the powerful lessons we can learn from the art of archery. Just as an archer carefully aims their arrow, please help us to set our sights on You and align our lives with Your will. When we miss the mark, please remind us of Your endless grace and the new opportunities You provide to improve and grow. Teach us to trust in Your guidance, knowing that with You, every shot we take can bring us closer to the life You've designed for us. May our actions, decisions, and words be like arrows that fly true, bringing glory to Your name. In Jesus' mighty name, we pray, Amen.

Fun Fact: Archery - Ancient Precision, Modern Safety

Did you know that when you pick up a bow, you're stepping into a tradition that dates back thousands of years? Archery is one of the oldest skills known to humankind, but here's the kicker—it's also one of the safest sports you can practice today! According to the National Safety Council, archery is even safer than golf, with fewer injuries reported per participant. Imagine that—handling a bow and arrow, a weapon that once determined the fate of battles and empires, is now a sport where safety is king! But it doesn't stop there. Modern archers, like those ancient warriors, still rely on the same blend of focus, precision, and respect for the craft. Every time you nock an arrow and draw back that bowstring, you're not just aiming for the bullseye—you're connecting with a history rich in tradition, skill, and respect for the power you hold in your hands. How cool is that?

Creative Corner

CRAFT YOUR
FAITH ARROW

Craft an arrow that symbolizes your incredible faith journey and God's guidance. Display it proudly as a powerful reminder of the path you're on, guided by faith.

WHAT YOU NEED:

- A stick, chopstick, dowel, or straw for the shaft
- 3 feathers, leaves, or paper to craft your fletchings
- Glue, tape, or string
- Markers or paint

LET'S CRAFT:

1. <u>Prepare the Shaft</u>: Find a stick, chopstick, dowel, or straw. This will serve as the shaft of your arrow.
2. <u>Decorate the Shaft</u>: Using markers or paint, decorate the shaft with symbols, verses, or words that are meaningful to your faith journey.
3. <u>Create and Attach Fletchings</u>: If using feathers, attach them evenly spaced at one end of the shaft using glue, tape, or string. If making paper fletchings, cut out feather shapes from paper, decorate as desired, and then attach them similarly at one end of the shaft.
4. <u>Form the Nock</u>: At the end with the fletchings, make a small notch or cut on the edge of the shaft. This simulates where the arrow would attach to a bowstring.

Day 5

Axes of Transformation

Scripture Spotlight

"HE WILL SET HIS BATTERING ENGINES AGAINST YOUR WALLS, AND WITH HIS AXES HE WILL BREAK DOWN YOUR TOWERS."
EZEKIEL 26:9

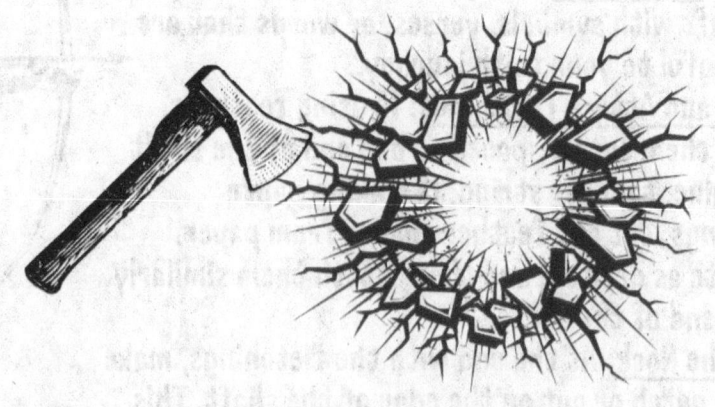

The Power of the Axe

Welcome to Day 5 of our *Weapons of the Bible* series. Today, we take a sharper look into the world of the axe. It's a powerful tool of both creation and destruction. In the prophecy against Tyre, the axe becomes a symbol of judgment and transformation, revealing the dual nature of God's interventions—both to dismantle and to rebuild. The siege of Tyre, with its battering rams and axes, showcases not only the physical might of armies but also the deeper spiritual significance behind the destruction of walls and towers long considered invincible.

The Axe in Action

In ancient warfare, axes were not only tools but extensions of a warrior's arm. Their design varied significantly, with some axes featuring long handles for swinging with two hands, maximizing the force to break down enemy defenses or combatants. Others were lighter and shorter, perfect for quick, one-handed strikes in close combat or even for throwing as a ranged weapon. The axe's versatility made it a formidable tool in sieges, able to hack through wooden defenses, splinter shields, and even cripple the wheels of chariots, disrupting enemy forces' mobility.

During the siege of Tyre, the Babylonians likely wielded a variety of axes. These ranged from heavy, broad-bladed axes for smashing through gates and walls, to lighter, sharper versions for precision tasks like cutting ropes or dismantling structures piece by piece. The mention of axes alongside battering rams in the siege highlights their pivotal role in breaching the city's defenses, symbolizing the unstoppable force of divine judgment through the hands of conquerors.

Lessons from the Lumber

In the Bible, the axe is often used as a symbol of God's judgment and the need for repentance, cutting away what is unproductive or sinful. This dual role—as a tool for both creation and destruction—mirrors our spiritual journey. Just as an axe can clear away dead wood or unfruitful trees, making space for new growth, God's work in our lives sometimes involves removing prideful barriers or harmful habits to make way for spiritual growth.

The same qualities that make an axe effective in battle—sharpness, weight, and strength—also remind us of the tough but necessary changes we need to make to follow God's will. When we think about the axe's role in the siege of Tyre, we see that real change often starts by breaking down the walls we've built around ourselves that stop us from growing. Whether it's letting go of bad habits, wrong beliefs, or sins that hold us back, God's word is like a mighty axe—sharp enough to penetrate precisely where it needs to, heavy enough to reach our deepest issues, and strong enough to withstand anything. It's the ultimate tool, perfectly crafted to reshape us into the people He wants us to be.

Let's Chat:

- What walls have you built that need to be taken down?

- Can you recall a time when removing something made a positive difference?

Prayer:

Lord, as we reflect on the role of axes as tools and symbols, please help us to identify and tear down any walls we've built that distance us from Your will. Please grant us the wisdom and courage needed for this kind of removal, trusting that You will reshape us and guide us to serve in Your kingdom. In Jesus' name, Amen.

Fun Fact: The Epsilon Axe of Biblical Times

Did you know? One of the most intriguing weapons from ancient history is the Epsilon axe. Though not mentioned directly in the Bible, this distinctive axe, named for its resemblance to the Greek letter 'Epsilon' (ε), was used during biblical times and features a curved blade that made it exceptionally versatile. Originally designed for woodcutting, the Epsilon axe became a formidable tool in combat. Its dual-purpose design—perfect for both hacking and pulling—made it a feared and respected weapon on the battlefield. Next time you see an axe, remember, you're looking at a tool with a history as sharp and versatile as its blade!

Creative Corner

AXE THROWING CHALLENGE

CREATE AN AXE WORTHY OF THROWING!

Materials Needed:
- Cardboard or thick foam sheets
- Scissors
- Paints or markers
- Glue or tape
- Foam, cardboard, or a sturdy stick (for the axe handle)

INSTRUCTIONS:

Design Your Axe Head: Draw an axe head shape on a piece of cardboard or foam sheet.

Cut and Decorate: Carefully cut out the axe head shape. Decorate both sides with paints or markers to add details like edges and designs for an authentic look.

Prepare the Handle: Smooth the foam, cardboard, or stick. If using a stick, sand down any rough edges to make it safe.

Assemble Your Axe: Attach the axe head to the handle using glue or tape. Ensure it's securely attached and let it dry.

AXE-THROWING STATION

Materials Needed:
- Soft objects for targets (toilet paper rolls, empty cardboard boxes, balloons)
- Masking tape or chalk
- Your crafted axe

INSTRUCTIONS:

Prepare Your Targets: Arrange soft objects to form a target. Ensure the setup is in a safe space where missed throws won't cause damage.

Mark Your Throwing Line: Use tape or chalk to mark a line on the ground for the thrower's stand.

Aim and Throw: Participants take turns standing behind the line, aiming their crafted axes at the targets, and tossing them to try and knock over the tower or pop a balloon.

SAFETY TIPS AND MORE:

- Always supervise children to ensure safe handling of materials and participation.
- Consider writing personal challenges such as pride, envy, or greed on your targets to symbolize overcoming them.

Day 6

The Spear of Victory

Scripture Spotlight

"HE KILLED A HUGE EGYPTIAN, AND THE EGYPTIAN HAD A SPEAR IN HIS HAND; BUT HE WENT DOWN TO HIM WITH A STAFF AND PLUCKED THE SPEAR OUT OF THE EGYPTIAN'S HAND, AND KILLED HIM WITH HIS OWN SPEAR." - 2 SAMUEL 23:21

The Emblem of Valor

Get ready for an action-packed Day 6 in our *Weapons of the Bible tour*, where we explore the spear—a weapon that's all about reach, flexibility, and raw courage.

Meet Benaiah, not just any warrior, but a legend whose bravery turned a desperate situation into a stunning victory. Faced with a giant Egyptian warrior armed with a spear, Benaiah, armed only with a staff, didn't back down. He courageously approached the giant, disarmed him by snatching the spear from his hand, and then used the very same spear to defeat the enemy. His incredible feat turned the battle on its head, ending it on his terms.

Legendary Spear Use

Imagine facing colossal dangers—beasts or foes—with nothing but a short sword. Tough, right? That's where the spear comes in, offering the reach you need to outmaneuver threats from a safe distance. Picture this: a roaring lion leaps towards you, but with a spear in hand, you stand your ground, untouchable. Now, picture Benaiah: outnumbered, out-weaponed, but not outwitted. He turns his desperate situation into a demonstration of agility and smarts, proving that sometimes, the best offense is a good defense... and a bit of bravery!

The Spear in Our Hands

Benaiah's thrilling story isn't just ancient history—it's a call to face our problems head-on: those towering challenges and fears that confront us. Like Benaiah, we might feel under-equipped, clutching at sticks against spears. Yet, his story reminds us that with God as our ally, our so-called weaknesses can transform into epic strengths. It's not the size of our arsenal but the depth of our faith and bravery that carves paths to victory.

Let's Chat:

- Have you ever felt like an underdog, only to find the strength you didn't know you had?

- Share a time when a challenge turned into a victory, with a little faith and maybe a daring move or two.

Prayer:

God, we're inspired by Benaiah's fearless spirit and the smart way he tackled his giant. Please ignite in us that same fire to confront our fears, not with the weapons of this world, but armed with faith in You. In Jesus' name, Amen.

Fun Fact: The Spear of Destiny

Have you ever heard of the Spear of Destiny? Also known as the Holy Lance, this artifact isn't just any old spear—it's steeped in legend and intrigue! It's believed to be the very spear that pierced Jesus's side during His crucifixion. Now, that's quite a piece of history!

While many tales swirl around the spear, suggesting it holds magical powers and can give unstoppable force to whoever possesses it, we know that any and all power comes from God alone. There's nothing magical or superstitious about it—the real power lies in faith. However,

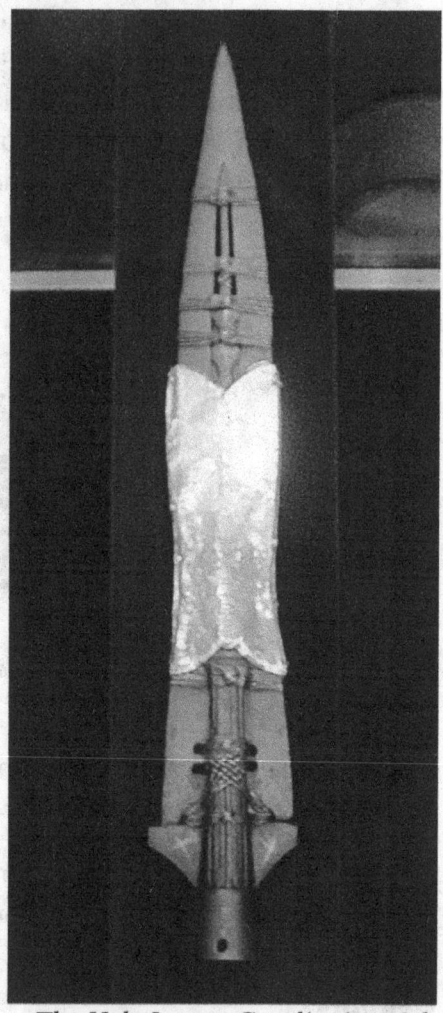

The Holy Lance, Carolingian, 8th century. Steel, iron, brass, silver, gold, leather. Length: 50.7 cm. Photo by Gryffindor, derivative work by Saibo. Licensed under CC BY-SA 3 .0.

the history and stories surrounding the spear are absolutely fascinating!

Over the centuries, all sorts of kings and rulers, including figures like Hitler, have sought after this legendary spear, drawn by its supposed divine or mystical properties. Imagine the allure of such an item, believed to shape the fate of its holder!

And here's another twist: there isn't just one spear. Several spears around the world claim to be the real Holy Lance, each housed in a notable location. You can find these spears in the Vatican, in Armenia's Echmiadzin Cathedral, in Poland, and in the Hofburg Palace in Vienna. This dispersal adds to the enduring allure and the mystery surrounding the spear's true origin and authenticity.

So, while we enjoy the thrilling tales of the Spear of Destiny, let's remember where true power and destiny really lie. Meanwhile, the quest for the spear continues to captivate the imaginations of history buffs, adventurers, and the curious all around the world. Who wouldn't want to explore these legends further?

Creative Corner

SPEAR ADVENTURES

POOL NOODLE SPEAR TOSS

Get ready for an epic spear toss challenge! Use spears made from pool noodles for a fun-filled game that tests your skill and accuracy.

Materials Needed:
- Pool noodles
- Scissors
- Colored tape or markers
- Hula hoops or laundry baskets (targets)
- Chalk

Instructions:

Prepare Your Spears:
1. Cut pool noodles into halves or thirds for shorter spears, or use them full-length.
2. Decorate with colored tape or markers.

Set Up Your Targets:
1. Arrange hula hoops at different heights and distances. Hang them from tree branches or play structures.
2. Place laundry baskets on the ground as 'spear dunk' targets.

Mark the Throwing Line:
3. Use chalk or sticks to make lines at varying distances.

Let the Games Begin:
4. Take turns throwing the spears, aiming to score by getting them through the hoops or into the baskets.
5. Keep score or just enjoy the fun!

SPEAR-INSPIRED SNACKS

Materials Needed:
- Cheese sticks or pretzel rods
- Sliced cucumbers or bell peppers
- Cream cheese or peanut butter
- Knife

Instructions:
1. Use cheese sticks or pretzel rods as the spear shaft.
2. Slice cucumbers or peppers into spearheads.
3. Attach the pieces with cream cheese or peanut butter and Enjoy!

Day 7

The Fire of Jericho

Scripture Spotlight

"They burned the city with fire, and all that was in it. Only they put the silver, the gold, and the vessels of bronze and of iron into the treasury of Yahweh's house."- Joshua 6:24

Welcome to the Grand Finale!

Here we are on Day 7, ready to blaze through our final discussion in the *Weapons of the Bible series*. Today's focus? Fire! We dive into the fiery tale of Jericho, a story that shows us God's overwhelming power and the beauty of following His lead. When Joshua and the Israelites encircled Jericho, obeying God's unique strategy, they witnessed the walls crumble—not just toppling a city but also purging what stood against God's will.

Fire: A Force of Cleansing and Enlightenment

Fire plays many roles in the Bible: a tool of destruction against foes, a symbol of God's awe-inspiring presence, and an agent of purification. Like the intense heat that refines gold, leaving behind only what's valuable, God sometimes guides us through "fire"—not literal flames, but tough situations that help make us stronger and get rid of the "dirt" in our lives, allowing us to shine more brightly.

The Cleansing of Jericho: A Fresh Start

Why did Jericho need to be consumed by flames? Picture your home cluttered with things that don't belong, distracting and obstructing peace. Jericho was like that—a place cluttered with practices and items that didn't align with God's design, needing a thorough cleanup. By commanding the city to be set aflame, God was doing a massive clean-up, clearing out the old to make way for something new and  pure, much like clearing your space to make it more joyful and useful.

Why This Matters to Us

This fiery story shines a light on the importance of choices and the power of letting go. It's about recognizing our "mess"—those habits or actions that aren't great for us—and deciding it's cleanup time. Just as a tidy room feels peaceful and welcoming, a life unburdened by unnecessary clutter—spiritual or otherwise—opens us up to joy and a deeper connection with God.

Let's Chat:

- Can you think of any habits or actions ("clutter") you might need to clear out of your life? How can we support each other in this big cleanup?

- Reflect on a time when something tough ("fire") helped polish and strengthen you. What did you learn from that experience?

Prayer:

Lord, thank You for the powerful lesson on fire. Help us to see the areas of our lives that need Your purifying flame. Please give us the strength to let go of what holds us back and the courage to embrace the change You bring. May our lives reflect Your purity and love, shining brightly for those around us. In Jesus' name, we pray. Amen.

Fun Fact: The Mesmerizing Dance of Fire

Ever wonder why fire dances in such mysterious shapes and forms? At the heart of every flame lies a trio of essentials: heat, fuel, and oxygen, known as the "fire triangle." Missing one, and the dance ends—the fire fades away. But here's where it gets truly captivating!

Imagine a fire in the vast, silent expanse of space. Without gravity's pull, flames don't leap and flicker; they transform into glowing, spherical orbs. Aboard the International Space Station, in the realm of microgravity, fire tells a different tale. It burns more leisurely and with less oxygen, casting a serene, round, blue glow that defies the earthbound image of a yellow, teardrop flame.

Firenado

But wait, there's more! Here on Earth, fire can whip up a whirlwind of awe. Picture this: fire tornadoes—yes, tornadoes made of fire! These swirling spectacles of nature's fury happen when intense heat and wild winds join forces, spinning flames up to dizzying speeds of 200 miles per hour and towering heights of 1,000 feet into the sky.

Fire, in all its forms—from the serene spheres of space to the tempestuous twisters on Earth—never ceases to amaze. It's a vivid reminder of the elemental power and unpredictable beauty that fire holds, captivating our imaginations and drawing us into its mesmerizing dance.

Creative Corner

FLAMES AND RENEWAL

JERICHO CLEANUP CHALLENGE

Mission: Transform a mundane cleanup into an exciting family adventure! Team up to conquer clutter and bring a fresh spark to your home.

Choose Your "Jericho": As a family, pick your "Jericho"—a cluttered room, chaotic garage, or overgrown garden. Each member suggests a spot, and together, decide on the cleanup conquest.

Supplies for the Siege: Cleanup tools: Brooms, mops, trash bags.

The Battle Plan:
1. The Trumpet Call: Start with a pep talk to get everyone ready. Share how this is about teamwork and transformation.
2. Seven Rounds: Mimic the seven-day march around Jericho by dividing the cleanup into seven "rounds" (15-minute intervals or different tasks).
3. The Shout: At the end of each round, shout together or make a joyful noise with cheers or party horns.

Post-Cleanup Celebration:
1. Decorate Your New Jericho: Everyone suggests ways to make the area more enjoyable.
2. Feast of Victory: Celebrate with a special treat or meal and discuss the experience.

ORANGE FIREWORKS!
Let's Get Fired Up with an Experiment!

What You Need:
- An orange
- A candle
- Lighter or matches (for adults)
- Water in a bowl (safety first!)

Steps:
1. Adults, it's showtime! Light the candle and place it safely on a table.
2. Peel the orange to get big pieces of skin.
3. Hold a piece of peel about an inch from the candle flame. Squeeze it firmly with the orange skin facing the flame and... POW! Watch the mini fire burst!

WHY IT'S COOL:

The orange peel contains a natural oil called limonene, which is highly flammable. When you squeeze the peel, it sprays this oil into the flame, causing a mini burst of fire!

CHAPTER 4
MIRACLES OF JESUS

Experience a Few of His Many Outstanding Miracles!

"RAISING OF LAZARUS"
GIOVANNI BENEDETTO CASTIGLIONE (GRECHETTO)
(ITALIAN, GENOA 1609–1664 MANTUA)

Day 1

Turning Water into Wine

Scripture Spotlight:

"Jesus said to them, "Fill the water pots with water." So they filled them up to the brim. He said to them, "Now draw some out, and take it to the ruler of the feast." So they took it. When the ruler of the feast tasted the water now become wine, and didn't know where it came from (but the servants who had drawn the water knew), the ruler of the feast called the bridegroom" - John 2:7-9

Party Panic!

Welcome to the first day of our series on the *Miracles of Jesus*, where we're exploring some of His most astonishing acts. Today, we splash into the miracle of turning water into wine! Imagine you're at a wedding celebration, and halfway through, the drinks run out—a major party foul, right? Back in Jesus' time, running out of wine at a wedding was even more serious; it could  bring great embarrassment to the hosting family. So, the pressure was on, when Jesus and His family attended a wedding in Cana where the wine was running low. Let's continue reading and see how Jesus addressed this potentially disastrous social blunder!

Jesus to the Rescue!

 Jesus' mom, Mary, knew her son could do something about the wine crisis. Even though Jesus said His time to show miracles hadn't started, He didn't want to see the family in trouble. So, He did something awesome. He told the servants to fill up some big jars with water. But these weren't just any jars—they were for special ceremonies, and they were huge!

Then, something epic happened. When the servants poured the water out for the master of the banquet, it wasn't water anymore—it had turned into the best wine of the night! Can you imagine the look on their faces? Jesus saved the party and made it even better than before!

Why This Miracle Rocks

This wasn't just about keeping the party going. This miracle shows that Jesus cares about all our problems, big or small. And it wasn't just about turning water into wine—it was about showing us that Jesus can take our ordinary stuff (like plain old water) and turn it into something amazing (like top-shelf wine).

Let's Chat:

- Have you ever seen something ordinary turn into something awesome? Maybe a simple project that turned out really great, or a small idea that became a fun adventure?

- What 'plain water' can you offer to Jesus this week? Think about the simple things in your life that you can give to Jesus, like helping out at home, or being nice to someone difficult.

Prayer:

Dear God, thank You for showing us that You're there in our fun times and our not-so-fun times. Please help us to remember that You can take even our ordinary, everyday stuff and make it amazing. Please give us the courage to bring our 'water' to You and watch You work, turning it into 'wine' that makes our days brighter and better. In Jesus' name, Amen.

Fun Fact: A Historic Find in Cana

Nazareth

Did you know that an archaeologist has found pieces of pottery she believes came from Cana, the very place where Jesus performed His first recorded miracle? During a salvage dig in the area between Nazareth and Capernaum, Israeli archaeologist Yardena Alexander uncovered fragments of large stone jars. These jars closely resemble the type described in the Gospel of John, used by Jesus to turn water into wine.

Moreover, American archaeologists excavating another site several miles to the north have also discovered pieces of stone jars from the time of Jesus. These intriguing finds leave us wondering: Could one or both of these sites actually contain the pottery from Jesus' first miracle?

CREATIVE CORNER
COLOR-CHANGING RICE NOODLES

INGREDIENTS

- Rice noodles (any shape will work)
- Purple cabbage
- Water
- Lemon juice or white vinegar
- Optional: other vegetables for garnish and flavor (like carrots, cucumbers, and bell peppers)

THE SCIENCE BEHIND IT

When you cook rice noodles in purple cabbage water, they soak up a special pigment called anthocyanin. Here's the fun part: squeeze lemon juice or vinegar over the noodles, and watch them change from blue to pink! The acid in the juice or vinegar changes the pH, causing this awesome color shift.

It's like a delicious science experiment on your plate!

INSTRUCTIONS

1. Prepare the Cabbage Water:
   - Chop half of a purple cabbage into chunks and place them in a large pot.
   - Cover the cabbage with plenty of water (enough to boil the noodles later).
   - Bring the water to a boil, then simmer for about 30 minutes until the water becomes deeply colored (a vibrant purple).
   - Strain out the cabbage pieces, keeping the purple cabbage water.

2. Cook the Noodles:
   - Bring the purple cabbage water back to a boil.
   - Add the rice noodles to the boiling cabbage water. Cook according to the package instructions until the noodles are tender.
   - Drain the noodles, but do not rinse them, to maintain the color.

3. Color Change Magic:
   - Serve the noodles hot or let them cool.
   - When you're ready to eat, squeeze some lemon juice or drizzle white vinegar over the noodles and watch them change from blue to pink! This happens because the acid (lemon juice or vinegar) changes the pH of the purple cabbage pigment in the noodles.

4. Serve and Enjoy:
   - Garnish with your choice of vegetables or add them to the cooking process for a more flavorful dish.
   - Optionally, you can also add a protein like chicken, shrimp, or tofu to make it a full meal.

Day 2

Feeding the 5000 - A Miracle of Provision

Scripture Spotlight

"Jesus took the loaves, and having given thanks, he distributed to the disciples, and the disciples to those who were sitting down, likewise also of the fish as much as they desired." - John 6:11

Super-Sized Snack

Hey everyone! Get ready for an awesome day on our journey through the *Miracles of Jesus*. Today, we're getting a little taste of the epic story of how Jesus turned a kid's small lunch into a mega feast for a huge crowd. Imagine this: over 5,000 people gathered on a hillside, hungry and waiting for something amazing to happen. They had no idea that Jesus was about to perform a miracle so incredible that we're still talking about it today!

Crowd Control

Picture us there, squished in a crowd, trying to catch a glimpse of Jesus. It's noisy, and everyone's shoulders are bumping. Then, we're told to sit down in groups. As everyone settles down, it gets quiet enough to hear Jesus speak. Every word He says is so fascinating that you just want to listen to Him forever.

As the day goes on, our stomachs start rumbling—loudly! But no one wants to leave; Jesus' words are too great to miss. They're filling us up in a way we didn't even know we needed, like quenching a thirst we didn't realize we had.

Mind-Blown!

Then, a kid walks up and gives his lunch to Jesus—just five loaves and two fish. Jesus takes it, gives thanks for it, and starts breaking it apart. Here's where it gets wild: He keeps breaking it, and the disciples start handing it out. It reaches everyone, even us in the back! And guess what? There's more than enough for everyone!

Everyone's eating, and there's still food left over—twelve whole baskets! All from just a boy's lunch! We're all thinking, "What? How?" This is the moment we realize something huge: not only are we no longer hungry, but our spirits are super full too. We just saw something impossible happen right in front of our eyes! Right there, with the grass under us and the sky above, it hits us—Jesus is the real deal, the One everyone's been waiting for!

Let's Chat:

- Can you think of a time when you felt like you didn't have enough—whether it was food, time, energy, or something else? Even though we may not always see miracles in a big way, God is right there with us. Did you reach out to Him in that situation?

- How can you share what you have with others this week, even if it seems small or not very important? Like the boy with his lunch, what could you offer that might help someone else, even in a small way?

Prayer:

Dear Lord, today we talked about how You took a little and turned it into a lot! Thank You for showing us that with You, there's always enough for everyone. Please help us to trust You more, especially when things look impossible, and teach us to share like the boy who gave his lunch. Please help us to remember that You're always there to fill our hearts with Your amazing love. In Jesus' name, Amen.

Fun Fact: The Humble Barley Loaves

Did you know the bread the boy shared with Jesus was made of barley? In Jesus' time, barley was considered the food of the poor—often fed to animals or used by those who couldn't afford the more desirable wheat bread. Barley bread was rough, coarse, and more commonly used for sustenance rather than luxury. The loaves Jesus used in this miracle were likely small, flat, and similar to personal-sized pita bread, a far cry from the large, fluffy loaves we see in stores today.

Mosaic of the Byzantine church at Tabgha- Near Sea of Galilee

What makes this detail even more incredible is that barley, though modest and simple, was transformed by Jesus into a feast for thousands. By using barley loaves for this miracle, Jesus demonstrated that even the simplest, most humble resources can become extraordinary when placed in God's hands. So, next time you think your contribution is too small to matter, remember the tiny barley loaves at the Feeding of the 5,000—small in size, humble in origin, but huge in impact!

CREATIVE CORNER
MIRACLE LOAVES

INGREDIENTS
- 2 cups of barley flour (all-purpose or whole wheat flour can also be used)
- 1 teaspoon of yeast
- 1 tablespoon of honey
- 1 tablespoon of olive oil
- 3/4 cup of warm water

NOT QUITE FOR 5000!
While we're not going to feed 5000 people, we can still bake our own mini barley loaves and get a taste of history! This fun activity lets you see the size and simplicity of the bread from Jesus' miracle, giving you a hands-on experience of ancient culinary practices.

INSTRUCTIONS
Prepare the Dough:
1. In a large bowl, mix water, yeast, honey, and oil. Let it sit for 10 minutes.
2. Add flour and mix until a dough forms.

Knead the Dough:
3. Turn the dough onto a floured surface.
4. Knead for about 5 minutes until smooth and elastic. Add a little flour if too sticky or water if too dry.

First Rise:
5. Place the dough back in the bowl and cover with a damp cloth.
6. Let it rise in a warm place for about 1 hour until doubled in size.

Shape the Loaves:
7. Punch down the risen dough to release air bubbles.
8. Divide into small portions and shape into small, flat rounds.

Bake the Loaves:
9. Preheat the oven to 375°F (190°C).
10. Place loaves on a baking sheet and bake for 15-20 minutes until golden brown.

SHARE AND ENJOY!

Day 3

Walking on Water

Scripture Spotlight:

"In the fourth watch of the night, Jesus came to them, walking on the sea. When the disciples saw him walking on the sea, they were troubled, saying, 'It's a ghost!' and they cried out for fear. But immediately Jesus spoke to them, saying, 'Cheer up! It is I! Don't be afraid.'"
- Matthew 14:25-27

Stepping into the Impossible

Welcome back as we continue to explore the incredible *Miracles of Jesus*. Today, we set our sails on the stormy seas of Galilee, where Jesus performed one of His most astounding miracles—walking on water. This wasn't just a display of divine power; it was a profound lesson in faith and trust.

Facing the Storm

In the middle of the night, the disciples found themselves in a boat battered by waves. They were tired, scared, and struggling against the storm. Suddenly, they saw a figure approaching them on the water. They thought it was a ghost! But it was Jesus, calmly walking toward them over the raging sea.

His presence on the water is a powerful reminder that He is Lord over all creation, including the wind and waves. His first words to the terrified disciples were a call to courage and a reminder of His care: "It is I. Don't be afraid." Responding with bold faith, Peter called out, "Lord, if it is you, command me to come to you on the waters." Jesus simply replied, "Come!" With that, Peter stepped out of the boat and walked on the water toward Jesus. But when he shifted his focus to the storm, he started to sink and cried out for help. Immediately, Jesus stretched out His hand, took hold of him, and said, "You of little faith, why did you doubt?"

The Miracle Into Our Lives

Life sometimes feels like a wild storm at sea, doesn't it? Maybe it's a huge project that feels overwhelming, a mis-understanding that seems too big to fix, or even just one of those days when nothing seems to go right. It's like we're stuck in that boat with the disci-ples, waves crashing around us, making everything feel out of control. But here comes the exciting part—Jesus is right there in the storm. When we turn our focus to Him, suddenly, the waves don't seem that scary. So, the next time you feel like you're sinking, remember Peter. Yes, he started to sink when he took his eyes off Jesus, but as soon as he cried out for help, Jesus was there to grab his hand. And guess what? He's there to grab yours too!

Let's Chat:

- Can you think of a time when life felt out of control, like a storm?

- How can you keep your focus on Jesus, just as Peter did initially, even when things get tough?

Prayer:

Jesus, thank You for the powerful lesson of faith that You taught us through Your miracle of walking on water. Help us to step out in faith, keeping our eyes fixed on You, even when the storms of life surround us. Please strengthen our trust in You, knowing that You are always there to catch us when we stumble. In Your name, we pray. Amen.

Fun Fact: The Jesus Lizard

Did you know there's a lizard nicknamed the "Jesus Lizard" because it can walk on water? Officially known as the Basilisk lizard, this amazing creature is found in the rainforests of Central and South America. When threatened, the Basilisk lizard can sprint on its hind legs and dash across the surface of rivers and ponds without sinking. This incredible ability comes from its specially designed feet, which have flaps of skin that open up and create more surface area, helping the lizard to stay above water. Just like Jesus astonished His disciples by walking on water, the Jesus Lizard amazes anyone who sees it in action with its miraculous ability to race across water.

CREATIVE CORNER
WALKING ON OOBLECK

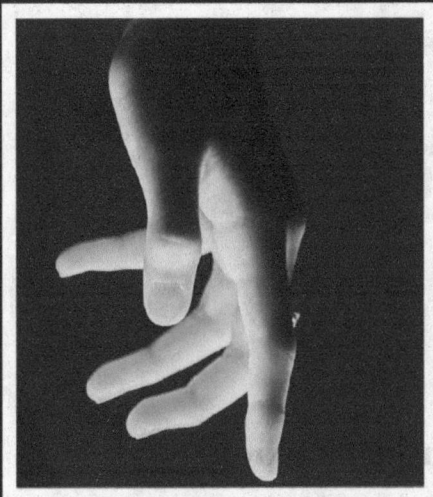

INGREDIENTS

- A large, shallow tray or baking dish
- Water
- Cornstarch
- Food coloring (optional)

FINGER-WALKING FUN!

Have you ever imagined walking on water like Jesus? Today, we're going to create something that lets your fingers do the walking on a miraculous substance called "oobleck"! Oobleck is a non-Newtonian fluid, which means it acts like a liquid when moved slowly but feels solid when you apply pressure quickly. Ready for some scientific fun?

INSTRUCTIONS

Create Your Oobleck:

1. Fill a tray halfway with water.
2. Gradually mix in cornstarch until it becomes a thick paste (Tip: This requires a lot of cornstarch, so start with a small amount of water and adjust as needed).
3. Optional: Add a few drops of food coloring.

Finger-Walking Challenge:

4. Lightly tap the surface with your fingers. It should feel solid.
5. Quickly 'walk' your fingers across the surface. Can they cross without sinking?
6. Move fast and see if you can go from one side of the tray to the other without getting stuck!

Optional: The Full Experience:

7. For more fun, pour the oobleck into a large baking tray.
8. Try stepping quickly across it. Speed and confidence are key —just like when Jesus walked on water!

Day 4

Opening Ears and Loosening Tongues

Scripture Spotlight:

"They were astonished beyond measure, saying, 'He has done all things well. He makes even the deaf hear and the mute speak!'" - Mark 7:37

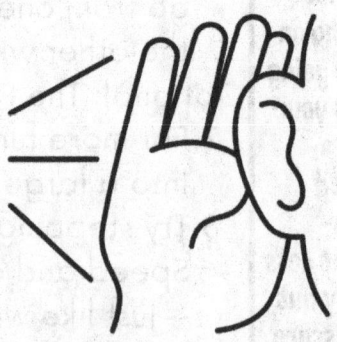

A Touch and a Word

Welcome back to our journey through the *Miracles of Jesus*. Today, we focus on a spectacular and unique miracle where Jesus heals a man who couldn't hear or speak. This isn't just a story of miraculous healing—it's a powerful demonstration of Jesus' intimate and personal approach to each individual's needs.

"Ephphatha!"—Be Opened!

In the bustling world of Galilee, one man lived in silence, isolated from the conversations and connections most take for granted. When Jesus met this man, He did something unexpected and, frankly, a bit shocking to our modern sensibilities. He put His fingers into the man's ears, then, spitting, touched the man's tongue. Imagine the crowd's anticipation and the man's initial shock.

With these actions, Jesus was doing more than just physical healing; He was communicating in a way that the man could understand—through touch. Then, looking up to heaven, Jesus sighed deeply, showing His empathy for the man's plight, and commanded, "Ephphatha!" which means "Be opened!" Immediately, the man's ears were opened, his tongue was released, and he began to speak clearly.

Astounding the Masses

The crowd's reaction was one of overwhelming amazement. They exclaimed, "He has done all things well!" Indeed, Jesus not only healed the man but did so with deep care and respect.

Applying the Miracle to Our Lives Today

Similarly, in today's fast-paced world, it's easy to feel like just another face in the crowd, unnoticed in a sea of many. Yet, just like in the story of Jesus healing the deaf man, we are reminded of His tender compassion and how He cares for each person's specific needs. Just as Jesus tailored His approach to meet that man's needs, He meets us where we are, attending to His sheep and caring for our unique challenges and situations. We are invited to build a personal relationship with Him, one that grows deeper through prayer.

Let's Chat:

- How can you show compassion or care to someone in your life this week, just like Jesus did for the deaf man?

- Can you recall a moment when an act of kindness made a big difference in your life?

Prayer:

Heavenly Father, thank You for showing us through Jesus' miracle how You care about every detail of our lives. Please teach us to use our hands and hearts to serve those around us in ways that honor You. Help us to be open to Your will in our lives, breaking down the barriers that keep us from hearing Your words and speaking Your truths. In Jesus' name, Amen.

Fun Fact: Super Sensitive Sound Detection

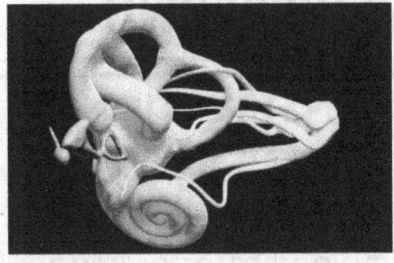

Inner ear

Did you know that our ears are like super-powered audio detectors? They are amazingly complex and can pick up sounds ranging from the softest murmur of leaves fluttering in the breeze to the thunderous roar of a jet engine soaring overhead. And get this—they can distinguish among approximately 400,000 different sounds! These wonders of human biology aren't just cool—they reveal the incredible intricacy of God's creation and help us truly appreciate the miracle when Jesus restored a man's hearing and speech.

Imagine what it would be like to never have heard a single sound and then, suddenly, your ears open, allowing you to witness the world you've always known in a completely new way. It's an unimaginable experience—stepping out of silence and into a vibrant world of sound. This powerful moment reminds us of the incredible, life-changing impact of Jesus' miracles.

CREATIVE CORNER
SILENT SIGNALS SHOWDOWN

MATERIALS:

- Paper
- Pens or markers
- Flashcards or paper for writing simple phrases or drawing images

COMICAL COMMUNICATION!
Get ready for a fun family game! Use non-verbal cues to communicate and guess messages written on flashcards. This game highlights the power of non-verbal communication and teaches patience and empathy. If you know sign language, try playing by only acting out the phrases.

INSTRUCTIONS

Create Flashcards:
- Prepare flashcards with simple phrases or images.

Game Setup:
- Gather everyone in a comfortable space.
- Shuffle and place the flashcards face down.

Playing the Game:
1. Each participant draws a card and acts out the phrase or image using only gestures —no speaking!
2. Others guess the phrase as quickly as possible.
3. Optional: Use a timer for added excitement.

Scoring (Optional):
- Award one point for each correct guess. The player with the most points wins.

Discussion:
- Discuss which phrases were hardest to guess and why.
- Talk about how it felt to communicate without words.

Day 5

Calming the Storm

Scripture Spotlight:

"And he awoke and rebuked the wind and said to the sea, 'Peace! Be still!' And the wind ceased, and there was a great calm." - Mark 4:39

Riding Roaring Waves

Welcome back as we continue our journey through the *Miracles of Jesus*. Today, strap in as we board a small boat with Jesus and His disciples, traveling across the Sea of Galilee. But this is no ordinary journey—we're about to find ourselves in the heart of a ferocious storm, experiencing firsthand the incredible power of Jesus to calm even the fiercest storm.

A Test of Faith

Imagine the cool evening air suddenly turning wild as fierce winds sweep across the sea. Waves crash over the sides of our modest boat, threatening to swallow it whole. The disciples are in a panic, water soaking their robes, fear clear in their eyes. In the middle of this crazy storm, Jesus remains asleep! As their fear reaches a peak, the disciples wake Him up and cry out, "Teacher, do you not care that we are perishing?"

The Calm After the Storm

Rising to His feet, Jesus faces the howling wind and towering waves. With a commanding voice that cuts through the thunderous noise, He declares, "Peace! Be still!" Suddenly, the chaos stops; the sea becomes as smooth as glass, and the wind turns into a gentle whisper. Turning to His disciples, Jesus asks them, "Why are you so afraid? Have you still no faith?" This moment is not just about stopping a storm—it's about awakening a deeper faith and understanding of who Jesus is.

Navigating Our Own Storms

Life can sometimes feel like a storm—wild, unpredictable, and beyond our control. But just as Jesus commanded the winds and waves to be still, He also has the power to bring stability to our lives. No matter what challenges we face, we can trust in Jesus' authority over all things and find security in His presence.

Let's Chat:

- Imagine being in that boat, witnessing this miracle. How would you feel seeing the storm cease at Jesus' command?

- How can recalling Jesus' power over the storm strengthen your trust in Him during these times?

Prayer:

Jesus, we are amazed by Your power and grateful for Your presence. Please remind us that You are always with us, capable of bringing peace where there is disorder. Please continue to strengthen our faith as we learn to trust and lean on You even when the winds and waves are crashing around us. In Your wonderful name, Amen.

Fun Fact: The Sea of Galilee

Did you know that the Sea of Galilee, where Jesus calmed the storm, is particularly known for its sudden and violent storms? Tucked below sea level, this relatively small lake, 13 miles long and 8 miles wide, is nestled 690 feet beneath sea level and is encircled by hills that tower up to 2,000 feet above its surface. This unique geographic bowl sets the stage for some mighty storms!

Here's what happens: As the warm, moist air from the water rises in the cool of the evening, it's rapidly replaced by cooler air tumbling down from the surrounding hills. This clash creates whipping winds that can churn the lake's waters in no time, leading to sudden and fierce storms. No science, human effort, or tools can change the fierce weather in an instant—only our mighty God can do that!

CREATIVE CORNER
STORM IN A JAR

INSTRUCTIONS

Prepare the Storm Jar:
1. Fill the jar three-quarters full with water.
2. Add a few drops of blue food coloring for a sea-like effect (optional).
3. Add a few drops of dish soap for swirling waves.

Add the Boat:
4. Carefully place your toy or homemade boat on the water surface.

Create the Storm:
5. Seal the jar tightly.
6. Gently shake the jar to create a swirling, churning storm. Watch as the boat battles the waves!
7. Shine a flashlight through the jar to illuminate the stormy waters.

Calm the Storm:
8. Set the jar down on a stable surface and stop moving it.
9. Watch in awe as the storm settles and the water calms, leaving the boat floating peacefully.
10. Discuss how this amazing transformation represents Jesus' command, "Peace! Be still!" and the immediate calming of the sea.

MATERIALS

- Large clear jar or transparent container
- Water
- Dish soap
- Blue food coloring (optional)
- Small toy boat or homemade boat (from cork or styrofoam)
- Small flashlight or lamp

CALM IN THE CHAOS!

Experience the thrill of creating and calming a storm, like Jesus did on the Sea of Galilee!

Day 6

Jesus Heals a Leper

Scripture Spotlight:

"WHILE HE WAS IN ONE OF THE CITIES, BEHOLD, THERE WAS A MAN FULL OF LEPROSY. WHEN HE SAW JESUS, HE FELL ON HIS FACE AND BEGGED HIM, SAYING, "LORD, IF YOU WANT TO, YOU CAN MAKE ME CLEAN." HE STRETCHED OUT HIS HAND AND TOUCHED HIM, SAYING, "I WANT TO. BE MADE CLEAN." IMMEDIATELY THE LEPROSY LEFT HIM." - LUKE 5:12-13

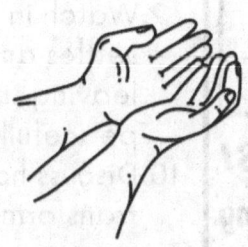

A Touch of Compassion

Welcome back as we continue our exploration of the *Miracles of Jesus*. Today, we approach a remarkable story of Jesus healing a man with leprosy. In ancient times, leprosy was not only a feared disease due to its physical effects but also because of the isolation that came with it. Those afflicted were required to stay away from others to prevent spreading the disease.

Meeting Jesus

Can you imagine being the man with leprosy? He wasn't allowed to be near others, and anyone who saw him would likely be afraid or look the other way. But when he saw Jesus, he was filled with hope and fell face down. He showed complete faith in Jesus' healing power by not asking if Jesus could heal him, but confidently declaring: "Lord, if you are willing, you can make me clean."

Jesus' Healing Hand

What Jesus did next was truly astonishing. He touched the man! Normally, no one would dare touch someone with leprosy because touching a leper was not only considered ceremonially unclean but there was also fear of contracting the disease. Jesus wasn't disgusted or afraid. He doesn't judge people by their disease or appearance; He looks at the heart. He simply said, "I am willing, be clean," and just like that, the man's leprosy was gone. Jesus' compassionate touch was a powerful act of acceptance, cleansing, and healing.

Today's Lepers

This miracle reminds us that no one is beyond the reach of God's love and healing power. Although we may not encounter someone with leprosy today, this story challenges us to reflect on how we treat those who are sick, outcasts, or considered untouchable by society. It also prompts us to reflect on how we view ourselves. No matter what people think or how alone a person may feel, God's deep love and compassion are for all.

Let's Chat:

- Can you think of ways we can show kindness to someone who feels left out or alone?

- How does it make you feel knowing that Jesus wants to help everyone?

Prayer:

Dear God, thank You for showing us through Your healing of the leper that no one is beyond Your compassion. Please help us to love like You, reaching out to those who are lonely, hurting, or rejected. Please teach us to see the unseen and to act with courage and compassion. In Jesus' name, Amen.

Fun Fact: Leprosy Through the Ages

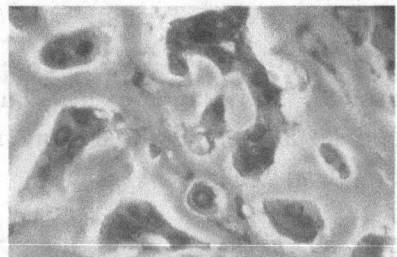

Pathological Sample Under a Microscope.

Did you know that leprosy, also known as Hansen's disease, is still around today? Caused

by the bacteria Mycobacterium leprae, leprosy was historically feared as a highly contagious and incurable disease, leading to the isolation of those affected to prevent its spread. In ancient times, communities would often separate people with leprosy, pushing them to live far from healthy populations.

Leprosy can impact the skin, nerves, eyes, and nose, and if left untreated, it may result in nerve damage, paralysis, blindness, and deformities of the hands and feet. No wonder people were terrified of catching it! Interestingly, what the Bible refers to as "leprosy" might not align perfectly with modern Hansen's disease. The term "leprosy" in biblical times was a catch-all used for various skin ailments or different diseases altogether, not just the leprosy we understand today.

The healing of a person with leprosy was a significant event, reversing not only physical symptoms but also restoring sight, mobility, and community connections. For someone branded as untouchable and living a life marred by humiliation and separation, being healed by Jesus was nothing short of a new life. Jesus' acts of healing leprosy were truly miraculous!

CREATIVE CORNER
CARDS OF COMPASSION

CARDS FOR WHAT?

Ever wanted to brighten someone's day but didn't know how?
Making encouraging cards for people in need is a fun way to spread joy and kindness!

WHY IT'S GREAT:

This activity taps into your creative skills and gives you a chance to make a real difference in someone's life. By sending a card, you're sharing a piece of your heart and showing someone that they are not alone and that someone cares. It's a powerful way to spread kindness and joy!

INSTRUCTIONS

Step 1: Pick the Recipient!
Do you know someone who could use a bit of encouragement today?
If yes, great! If not, no worries—there are many organizations that can help you send your cards to people in need.

Here are some awesome options:
- St. Jude Children's Hospital: Use their free e-card service to send cheerful messages to sick children. Visit www.stjude.org/get-involved/other-ways/send-an-ecard.html
- Braid Mission: They accept cards for foster kids, delivered on their birthdays or when they need a boost. Check them out at www.braidmission.org/cards-of-hope/
- Send a Smile Today: They welcome cards for cancer patients of all ages, especially adults. Learn more at https://sendasmiletoday.org/

Step 2: Design Your Card!
Whether it's a physical piece of paper, a store-bought card, or a free e-card, make it special. Write an uplifting message—think bright, cheerful, funny, or clever. Add a joke or draw a friendly picture to make it even more awesome!

Step 3: Send It!

Day 7

Raising Lazarus from the Dead

Scripture Spotlight:

"JESUS SAID TO HER, 'I AM THE RESURRECTION AND THE LIFE. HE WHO BELIEVES IN ME WILL STILL LIVE, EVEN IF HE DIES. WHOEVER LIVES AND BELIEVES IN ME WILL NEVER DIE. DO YOU BELIEVE THIS?'" JOHN 11:25-26

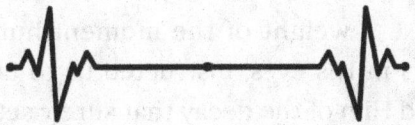

A Miracle of Life Over Death

Welcome back as we conclude our exploration of the *Miracles of Jesus* with one of the most breathtaking events recorded in the Bible—the resurrection of Lazarus. This isn't just a miracle; it's a powerful declaration of Jesus' mastery over the grave! Imagine being there, witnessing this moment firsthand. Let's explore this story as if from Martha's perspective, offering an interpretation inspired by her experiences.

From Martha:

By the time Jesus reached Bethany, Lazarus had been in the tomb for four days. Eager yet heartbroken, I went out to meet Him. Torn between grief and faith, I said, "Lord, if you had been here, my brother wouldn't have died. But I know that even now, whatever you ask of God, God will give you." Jesus' response was both comforting and challenging. He  promised Lazarus would rise again, affirming that He is the resurrection and the life, and asked if I believed in Him. Standing there, amidst my deepest sorrow, I confessed, "Yes, Lord. I believe that you are the Christ, God's Son, who is to come into the world."

The Tomb:

I quickly fetched Mary, and together we approached Jesus. Like me, Mary fell at His feet, expressing her grief that if He had been there, Lazarus would still be alive. Jesus, deeply moved and troubled, asked to see the tomb. As we stood by the cave with the stone still sealing it, the weight of the moment hung heavily upon us all. Jesus, with tears in His eyes, instructed us to take the stone away. Hesitant, I reminded Him of the decay that surely set in. Yet, He assured us we would see God's glory. With faith, we moved the stone away.

Come Out!

Then, with a commanding voice, Jesus called into the darkness, "Lazarus, come out!" What happened next was nothing short of miraculous. My brother, whom we had mourned and buried, emerged alive, still wrapped in his burial clothes. The mixture of joy, shock, and awe was overwhelming. In that moment, it became clear who Jesus truly was—not just a healer or teacher, but the master over life and death. Our understanding of what is possible was transformed forever.

The Impact on Us Today

 The story of Lazarus is more than an ancient tale; it speaks directly to us today. It reminds us that Jesus is present in our most desperate moments, offering hope when all seems lost. It's a reminder that He is moved by our tears and may even weep with us because He cares. Mirroring His own death and resurrection, this miracle illustrates that our difficulties and trials, even those that seem as final as death, are never beyond the reach of Jesus' power. Today, we can face our darkest hours with the assurance that Jesus has the power to bring life from death and light into any darkness.

Let's Chat:

- How does witnessing Jesus' power over death in the story of Lazarus change how you view your own challenges and trials?

- Think of a time when it seemed all hope was lost. How did faith play a role in overcoming that moment?

Prayer:

Lord, thank You for the powerful demonstration of Your victory over death. Please help us remember that with You, hope is never lost, and death is not the end. Strengthen our hearts to face life's hardest moments with courage and unwavering faith, anchored in Your promise of eternal life. Amen.

Fun Fact: Visiting Lazarus' Tomb Today

Did you know that you can still visit the tomb of Lazarus today? The site, believed to be the tomb of Lazarus, is located in the town of al-Eizariya, which is translated as "The Place of Lazarus" in Arabic. This town is situated on the West Bank and retains its historical and spiritual significance because it's identified with the biblical village of Bethany, where Jesus frequented and where He raised Lazarus from the dead.

Visitors to al-Eizariya can explore a traditional tomb cut from the rock, which is regarded as the place where Lazarus was laid to rest and miraculously brought back to life. The entrance to the tomb is through a steep set of steps leading down into a series of chambers, where pilgrims can actually enter and experience the intimate and ancient space that resonates with the biblical account of Lazarus' resurrection. To see more, check out a video about Lazarus' tomb by searching for "Exploring the Tomb of Lazarus in Bethany" on YouTube or typing youtu.be/Oa4 SMKvO5o4 into your browser.

CREATIVE CORNER
LAZARUS WRAP GAME

MATERIALS

- Rolls of toilet paper or cloth strips
- Timer
- A camera for pictures!

THATS A WRAP!

Get ready for some hilarious fun! Quickly wrap a family member in toilet paper or cloths to recreate the scene of Lazarus coming out of the tomb. Aim for the best and most secure wrapping. See who can create the most convincing Lazarus in record time!

INSTRUCTIONS

1. Form Teams:
   - If you have four or more players, divide into teams.
   - Select one team member to play the role of Lazarus.
2. Wrap Lazarus:
   - Set a timer for 3-5 minutes.
   - On "go," teams start wrapping their Lazarus in toilet paper or cloth strips.
   - Aim to cover Lazarus completely and creatively within the allotted time.
3. Race to the Finish Line (Variation):
   - After wrapping, have each Lazarus race to a predetermined finish line.
   - The first Lazarus to cross the finish line without losing their wrapping wins.
   - Ensure there's enough space and safety measures in place to prevent falls.
4. Judging:
   - If racing isn't feasible, judge based on creativity and completeness of the wrapping.
   - Determine a winner based on the best-dressed Lazarus.
5. For Smaller Groups:
   - With fewer than four participants, each player takes turns wrapping a Lazarus.
   - Use the timer to challenge each player to beat the best wrapping time or judge based on the quality of the wrap.

CHAPTER 5
EXTRAORDINARY BLESSINGS
TO ORDINARY PEOPLE
Discovering Incredible People with
Amazing Gifts

"SAMSON STANDS OVER VANQUISHED PHILISTINES"
FREDERIC SHIELDS (1833–1911)

Day 1

Samson's Miraculous Strength

Scripture Spotlight:

"SAMSON CALLED TO YAHWEH, AND SAID, "LORD YAHWEH, REMEMBER ME, PLEASE, AND STRENGTHEN ME, PLEASE, ONLY THIS ONCE, GOD, THAT I MAY BE AT ONCE AVENGED OF THE PHILISTINES FOR MY TWO EYES."" - JUDGES 16:28

A Hero is Promised

Welcome to an exciting start to our journey through the lives of ordinary people blessed in extraordinary ways by God! Today, we flex our muscles and explore the thrilling story of Samson, whose life was marked by a heavenly promise from the very beginning. Imagine a world where heroes are chosen even before birth—Samson's story begins just like that!

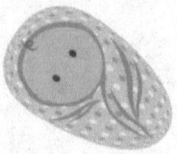

A Special Announcement

In a time when Israel was facing great troubles, an angel of the Lord brought incredible news to a woman who had never been able to have children. She and her husband, Manoah, were stunned to learn that not only would they have a son, but that he was destined for a special purpose from God. From birth, Samson was to be a Nazirite, set apart with specific rules to follow, including never cutting his hair. This vow was a sign of his dedication to God, who gave him immense strength.

The Power of a Promise

From tearing apart a lion with his bare hands to toppling entire buildings, Samson's strength was unmatched. But this incredible power was not just for showing off—it was given to him to protect and lead his people. Samson's life teaches us that with great gifts come great responsibilities. His strength was meant to be used wisely, in ways that honored the promise his parents made and the plans God had for him. However, Samson repeatedly broke the vows that were meant to set him apart. He touched dead bodies (like the lion's carcass), drank alcohol at feasts, and ultimately had his hair cut by Delilah while he was asleep—all actions that went against the vows he was supposed to keep.

Our Super Gifts

Despite his many poor choices, God still used Samson to deliver Israel from the Philistines. This teaches us that while we may make mistakes and fall short, God's purposes can still be accomplished through us. It also reminds us that our gifts and strengths should be used in alignment with God's will, and not for selfish gain. Samson's story encourages us to think about our greatest strengths, whatever they may be, and recognize that they are gifts from God. Whether you're really good at math, painting, or building, we all have special talents (even if you don't know what it is). As Christians, we are called to use these abilities not just for ourselves but to serve God and others. When we do, God can use our gifts for the greater good, helping to build His kingdom and make the world a better place.

Dive Deeper into Samson's Story

Read the whole story of Samson in Judges 13-16 as a family and see if you can spot the times Samson broke the Nazirite vows. Pay special attention to the promises made before his birth and how, despite his mistakes, God still used him to accomplish great things. Think about how we can apply these lessons to our own lives and what we can learn from this story.

Let's chat:

- What are some talents or strengths you see in yourself or in your family members? How can you use these gifts for good?

- Can you think about a time when you used a personal strength to help someone else?

Prayer:

Dear God, thank You for the amazing story of Samson and the reminder that You have a plan for each of us. Please help us to discover our own strengths and use them according to Your will. Guide us to be brave and wise in using our gifts, just as You intended when You gave them to us. Amen.

Fun Fact: The Power of the Nazirite Vow

Did you know that Samson's remarkable strength was linked to a special promise called the Nazirite vow? This vow, which you can explore in Numbers 6:1-21, was taken by individuals who dedicated themselves to God in an extraordinary way and involved several strict commitments:

- **Abstain from Wine and Vinegar:** Nazirites skipped all forms of alcohol and vinegar, keeping their bodies pure and ready for divine tasks.

- **Avoid Grapes and Grape Products:** They could not eat fresh grapes or raisins, nor consume grape seeds or skins.

- **Refrain from Cutting Hair:** Their uncut hair wasn't just for looks—it was a symbol of their commitment, visible to all. Their long locks of hair reminded everyone of their dedication to God.

- **Avoid Contact with the Dead:** Nazirites couldn't go near dead bodies, ensuring they stayed ritually clean.

- **Consecration and Rituals upon Completion:** Upon completing the vow period, Nazirites were to perform specific rituals at the Temple, including offering a lamb as a burnt offering, an ewe as a sin offering, and a ram as a fellowship offering, along with a basket of unleavened bread, grain offerings, and drink offerings.

After completing the vow, they had to shave their heads ceremonially at the entrance to the Tent of Meeting (or later, the Temple), signifying the end of their vow and their return to ordinary life. These rigorous practices highlighted their total dedication to God and set them apart in their communities, demonstrating their holy commitment through visible and practical actions.

Creative Corner

SAMSON'S STRENGTH CHALLENGE

Gear up for a fun challenge inspired by the story of Samson, exploring themes of strength and responsibility through exciting activities!

Materials Needed:

- Objects of varying weights (hand weights, books, cans of food, etc.)
- Stopwatch or timer
- Blindfold (optional)
- Rope or long piece of fabric (for tug-of-war)
- Activity score cards (to record each participant's performance)

HERE'S SOME IDEAS TO GET YOU STARTED:

Strength Relay:

1. Set up a course where participants must carry different objects from one point to another, from lightest to heaviest.
2. Each participant moves all items, one at a time, to the finish area.
3. Time each participant to see who completes the task the fastest.

Blindfold Challenge:

1. Inspired by Samson's time of blindness, participants complete a simple task blindfolded (like stacking cups or tying knots).
2. This illustrates overcoming challenges even when facing difficulties.

Tug-of-War:

1. Divide participants into two teams for a tug-of-war contest using a rope or long piece of fabric.
2. This game symbolizes the struggles and battles Samson faced.

Wrap it up: Celebrate with awards or prizes! Remember, while physical strength is valuable, strength of character and making wise decisions is even more important.

Day 2

David's Courage

Scripture Spotlight:

"BE COURAGEOUS, AND LET'S BE STRONG FOR OUR PEOPLE AND FOR THE CITIES OF OUR GOD; AND MAY YAHWEH DO WHAT SEEMS GOOD TO HIM.'" - 2 SAMUEL 10:12

A Hero's Journey of Courage

Welcome back to our inspiring journey through *Extraordinary Blessings to Ordinary People*. Today, we are swept into the epic adventures of David, whose life is filled with battles, moral challenges, and personal trials. From a young shepherd to the king of Israel, David's story is a testament to the power of courage in its many forms.

Defying Giants and Defending Principles

David's tale of courage begins with the legendary confrontation with Goliath in 1 Samuel 17, where a sling, a stone, and unshakable faith bring a giant to his knees. But as we read on, his bravery didn't stop at Goliath's fall. After this victory, David found himself in the service of King Saul, where his success on the battlefield and growing popularity began to spark Saul's jealousy. Saul, consumed by envy and fear of losing his throne, pursued David relentlessly, often seeking to kill him. Despite being hunted by the king, David had numerous opportunities to strike down his pursuer but chose the higher road—showing incredible courage in his restraint and respect for Saul as God's anointed king (1 Samuel 24).

Leadership, Lapses, and Lessons Learned

Ascending to the throne, David's courage took on a new dimension—leadership. Uniting the tribes of Israel and capturing Jerusalem required more than bravery in battle; it demanded vision and the courage to make bold decisions for the greater good (2 Samuel 5). However, David was not without faults. His grave mistakes brought him to his knees in a different kind of battle—a battle within. Guided by the prophet Nathan's rebuke, David's heartfelt repentance in Psalm 51 revealed the courage to admit his wrongs and seek redemption.

A King's Heartache and Hope

David's later years brought personal grief, especially through the betrayal and loss within his own family. One of the most painful moments was when his son Absalom, who had grown resentful and ambitious, led a rebellion against him. Absalom turned many people against David, attempting to overthrow his father and take the throne for himself (2 Samuel 15-18). Forced to flee from his own son, David's journey became a heartbreaking mix of fear, sorrow, and the courage to keep going. Despite Absalom's betrayal, David's deep love for his son never wavered, and he mourned deeply when Absalom was killed during the conflict. This chapter of David's life teaches us about the courage needed to navigate family heartbreaks and the complexities of love and forgiveness, even in the face of betrayal.

Our Courageous Journey

David's life is filled with moments that remind us we don't have to rely on our own strength. From standing up to giants to facing personal failures and difficult family situations, David's courage came from his trust in God. His story teaches us that true courage isn't about being the strongest or the bravest on our own—it's about leaning on God when we face battles, make hard choices, or feel overwhelmed by life's challenges. Just as David called on God for help, we too can find our strength in Him. No matter what is going on in life, we can always call out to our Father, and He hears our prayers, guiding us through every storm.

Let's Chat:

- How can you lead others with integrity (honesty and strong moral values)?

- How does David's courage in admitting his mistakes inspire you to address your own?

Prayer:

Heavenly Father, thank You for the lessons we continue to learn from David's life. Please help us remember his story and find the courage to stand against wrongdoing, lead with integrity, admit our faults, and handle personal trials bravely. May we find our strength in You and inspire courage in others through our actions and choices. In Jesus' name, Amen.

Fun Fact: Unearthing the Legacy of King David

Tel Dan Stele (Wikimedia Commons, 2017)

Did you know archaeologists have uncovered incredible clues to King David's existence? Here's a look at some of the exciting discoveries that helped confirm his place in history:

- **The Tel Dan Stele:** This ancient stone bears an inscription referring to the "House of David." Discovered in northern Israel in 1993, the Tel Dan Stele dates back to the 9th century BCE, providing real evidence of David's dynasty—how amazing is that?

- **The Mesha Stele:** Found in Jordan, this stone records the victories of King Mesha of Moab and also mentions the "House of David." It suggests that David was remembered as a legendary figure by his enemies, which adds even more to his historic impact!

- **City of David Archaeological Site:** Did you know you can walk through parts of ancient Jerusalem where David once ruled? Archaeologists continue to dig in the City of David, where they've uncovered structures, pottery, and even water systems that date back to David's reign. It's like stepping into a living museum of biblical history!

Creative Corner
COURAGEOUSLY EXPRESSING FAITH

David's Harmonious Legacy

David's harp playing was so soothing that he was summoned to play for King Saul to calm the king's troubled spirit (1 Samuel 16:23). He also authored many Psalms, showing his ability to express deep emotions through music and poetry.
He demonstrated real courage by confronting and expressing his deepest emotions.

Ignite Your Inner David

Taking inspiration from David, let's wholeheartedly express our feelings and praise God through art, poems, or music!

Optional Materials:

- Paper and pens for writing poems or drawing
- Musical instruments or music-making supplies
- Art supplies like paint, markers, or clay

Instructions:

1. Pick Your Creative Outlet: Decide whether you want to write a poem, make a drawing or painting, or create a piece of music.
2. Set the Theme: Pick a theme like gratitude, seeking guidance, overcoming challenges, or celebrating nature—just like in the Psalms.
3. Create: Spend some time crafting your piece. Let your thoughts and emotions flow freely. This isn't about perfection—it's about expression!
4. Share (Optional): If you're comfortable, share your creation with family or friends. Talk about what inspired you and how this activity helped you connect with David's way of worship and communicating with God.

JUMP INTO THIS FUN AND CREATIVE CHALLENGE, AND EXPRESS YOUR FAITH IN YOUR OWN UNIQUE WAY!

Day 3

Joseph's Wisdom

Scripture Spotlight:

'Pharaoh said to Joseph, "Because God has shown you all of this, there is no one so discreet and wise as you. You shall be over my house. All my people will be ruled according to your word. Only in the throne I will be greater than you."' - Genesis 41:39-40

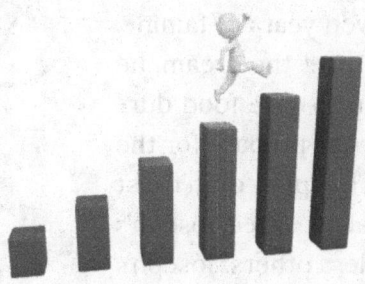

A Journey from Dreams to Deliverance

Welcome back as we continue our adventure through *Extraordinary Blessings to Ordinary People*. Today, we uncover the story of Joseph—a tale filled with dramatic twists, unexpected turns, and wisdom that carried him from the darkest of pits to the highest palace in Egypt. Joseph's incredible ability to interpret dreams wasn't just a special talent; it was a gift from God that would change the fate of an entire nation. (Genesis 37-50)

From Hardships to High Honors

Joseph's journey was far from easy. Betrayed by his brothers and sold into slavery (Genesis 37), he found himself in Egypt as a servant and later a prisoner (Genesis 39). Yet, Joseph didn't let his difficult circumstances define him. Instead, he leaned on God's guidance, using his wisdom in every challenge he faced. When Pharaoh needed someone to interpret his troubling dreams (Genesis 41), it was Joseph's faith-fueled insight that saved the day—and the nation. Suddenly, the once-forgotten prisoner was now second-in-command over all of Egypt!

Wisdom That Saves

In Pharaoh's dreams, Joseph saw both a warning and a solution: seven years of plenty followed by seven years of famine. But he didn't just interpret the dream; he devised a brilliant plan to save food during the abundant years to prepare for the tough times ahead. This plan didn't just secure Egypt's survival—it saved Joseph's own family and countless others. Joseph's wisdom wasn't just about knowing what to

do; it was about trusting God's plan and acting on it with courage and skill.

Applying Joseph's Lessons Today

Joseph's life reminds us that wisdom goes beyond just having knowledge—it's about using that knowledge in ways that honor God and help others. Even when life seems unfair or the future uncertain, Joseph's story encourages us to trust in God's bigger picture. His wisdom teaches us to see beyond our immediate problems and to work with faith toward a greater good.

Let's Chat:

- Can you think of a time when you faced a big challenge? What helped you get through it?

- What can we learn from Joseph about trusting God when things seem out of our control?

Prayer:

Heavenly Father, thank You for the inspiring story of Joseph, who used the wisdom You provided to interpret dreams and save nations. Please help us seek Your wisdom in our daily challenges and apply it as Joseph did, with both intelligence and faith. Teach us to manage the resources and responsibilities You've entrusted to us wisely, always mindful of Your greater plan. In all our decisions, please guide us to act justly and serve others selflessly. In Jesus' mighty name, Amen.

Fun Fact: The Mysterious Tomb in Egypt

 Did you know that archae-ologists have discovered a unique tomb in Egypt that stands out from tradition-al Egyptian burials? Locat-ed in Avaris, a region asso-ciated with the time of Joseph, this tomb differs from others because it was found empty of its original remains—its bones were removed long ago! This unusual detail has sparked curiosity among scholars who wonder if it could be con-nected to Joseph, who asked for his bones to be taken back to his homeland (Genesis 50:24-26), as described in the Bible.

Adding to the intrigue, a statue near the tomb de-picted a man with red hair wearing a multicolored coat—echoing the description of Joseph's famous "coat of many colors" (Genesis 37:3). While no definitive proof exists to confirm this is Joseph's tomb, the intriguing combination of missing bones and unique artifacts invites us to imagine the possibility that this site holds a link to one of the Bible's most extraordinary stories!

Creative Corner
GRAIN MASTER GAME

Can you crack the secret code of grains to demonstrate effective resource management and foresight?

Materials Needed:

- Paper and pencils for each player.
- A set of colored markers or pencils.

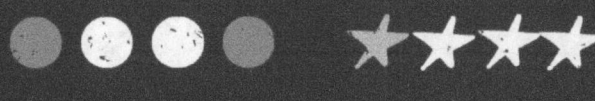 

SET UP:

- **Pick Your Resources:** Choose 4 colors to represent resources (like red for wheat, green for barley, yellow for corn, and blue for rice)
- **Code Maker:** One player secretly picks a sequence of 4 colors.
- **Code Breakers:** Others guess the sequence using hints.

HOW TO PLAY:

1. **Guessing:** Code Breakers Write down their guesses.
2. **Code maker gives feedback:** "Storage" (black star) for correct color and spot. "Harvest" (yellow star) for correct color, wrong spot.
3. **Code Breakers** use the hints to improve their guesses.
4. **Turns:** Guess, get feedback, and repeat until someone guesses the sequence.
5. **Winning:** First to guess the sequence wins and is the "Grain Master"!

Variations: Simplify with fewer colors or Increase the challenge with longer sequences.

Day 4

Esther's Bravery

Scripture Spotlight:

"FOR IF YOU REMAIN SILENT NOW, THEN RELIEF AND DELIV-
ERANCE WILL COME TO THE JEWS FROM ANOTHER PLACE, BUT
YOU AND YOUR FATHER'S HOUSE WILL PERISH. WHO KNOWS IF
YOU HAVEN'T COME TO THE KINGDOM FOR SUCH A TIME AS
THIS?"- ESTHER 4:14

A Queen's Courage

Today, we turn our attention to Queen Esther, whose remarkable bravery and self-sacrifice transformed her from an orphaned girl into a heroic queen of Persia. Faced with the impending destruction of her people, Esther's decision to act was not only bold but life-saving. Her courage shows us that standing up for what's right often involves risk, but with faith and preparation, we can make a difference.

The Challenge Before Her

When Esther learned of the decree to annihilate her people, she found herself uniquely positioned to help. Mordecai urged her to use her royal influence, but approaching King Xerxes without being invited could cost her life. Rather than acting impulsively, Esther paused to seek God's guidance. She called for a three-day fast, praying for strength and wisdom before taking the daring step to confront the king.

Courage in Action

After fasting and praying, Esther carefully planned her approach. She knew this decision wasn't just about bravery; it was about timing and strategy. She invited the king to a series of banquets, gradually building trust before finally revealing her identity as a Jew and pleading for her people's survival. Esther's actions teach us that courage sometimes involves waiting for the right moment and aligning our steps with God's will.

The Impact of Her Bravery

Esther's courage not only saved her people but also showed the importance of trusting God's plan even when the path seemed uncertain. She didn't rush into action but made sure her moves were grounded in prayer. This reminds us that real bravery isn't just acting in the moment—it's seeking God's direction and trusting Him to guide us. Esther's brave decisions changed history and remind us that we, too, can make a difference when we align ourselves with God's purpose.

Let's Chat:

- Is there someone in your life who could use encouragement to act bravely, like Mordecai did for Esther? How might you support them?

- How can Esther's example inspire you to act courageously for the good of your community?

Prayer:

Lord, thank You for the inspiring example of Queen Esther, who demonstrated bravery under pressure. Please help us to have courage in our lives to stand up for what's right, just as Esther did. Teach us to seek Your guidance first and to rely on You for wisdom and strength. May we face our challenges with bravery and faith, trusting in Your timing at every step. In Jesus' name, Amen.

Fun Fact: The Book of Esther and the Super Fun Festival of Purim

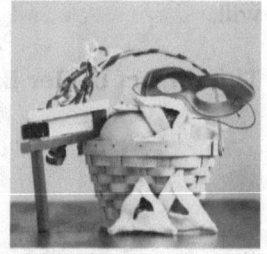

Hey, did you know that the Book of Esther is unique in the Bible because it doesn't even mention God's name? But don't let that fool you—it's packed with lessons of faith and helps readers see God's handiwork and presence behind the scenes, and it sparked one of the coolest holidays ever: Purim!

Purim isn't just any holiday—it's a Jewish celebration of the time Queen Esther saved her people in ancient Persia. During Purim, everyone gathers to listen to Esther's story, called the Megillah, and it's so interactive! Every time the bad guy Haman's name comes up, everyone boos and shakes noisemakers called "graggers" to literally blast his name away. It's like pressing the mute button during a commercial or cheering loudly to drown out something you don't want to hear.

But wait—it gets even better! Imagine a day where you can dress up as anything you want—from kings and queens to heroes and villains. That's Purim for you, complete with costumes, parties, and lots of laughter. Plus, everyone sends gift baskets filled with yummy treats to their friends. And in the spirit of kindness, people also give food or money to those in need, spreading happiness everywhere.

Purim is all about turning tough times into a chance for a giant, joyous party. It's about remembering how brave Esther was and celebrating with others. So, if you love stories about heroes, dressing up, and having fun, Purim is the festival for you!

Creative Corner

DIY GRAGGER

Get ready to make some noise!
Let's create our own graggers to shake every time we hear Haman's name while reading the Book of Esther.

HERE'S WHAT YOU'LL NEED:

- Empty plastic bottle with a lid
- Dried beans, rice, or small pebbles
- Stickers, colored paper, markers
- Tape or glue
- Optional: Streamers or ribbons

INSTRUCTIONS:

1. Prepare the Bottle: Clean and dry the plastic bottle.
2. Decorate Your Bottle: Use markers, colored paper, and stickers to make your bottle look amazing. You might want to draw symbols from Esther's story, write your name, or add streamers or ribbons to the neck for some fun flair.
3. Fill the Bottle: Fill the bottle one-quarter full with beans, rice, or pebbles for noise-making and secure the lid tightly, taping it if needed to keep it closed.
4. Shake and Test: Give your gragger a shake to test the sound.
5. Read and React: As you read the Book of Esther, shake your gragger like crazy every time Haman's name is mentioned. Let the noise-making begin and enjoy the fun!

Day 5

Ruth's Incredible Loyalty

Scripture Spotlight:

"RUTH SAID, "DON'T URGE ME TO LEAVE YOU, AND TO RETURN FROM FOLLOWING YOU, FOR WHERE YOU GO, I WILL GO; AND WHERE YOU STAY, I WILL STAY. YOUR PEOPLE WILL BE MY PEOPLE, AND YOUR GOD MY GOD." - RUTH 1:16

An Amazing Adventure of Loyalty

Hey there! Welcome back to our exciting journey through *Extraordinary Blessings to Ordinary People*. Today, we're gathering insights into the incredible story of Ruth, a true hero of loyalty, whose choices led to amazing adventures and helped shape history!

Choosing Friends Over Comfort

When Ruth's husband passed away, she faced a life-changing decision: stay in her familiar homeland of Moab or leave everything behind to support Naomi, her mother-in-law, in a strange new land. Staying in Moab would have been the comfortable choice—Ruth knew the customs, the people, and the language. But Ruth chose something radically different, to stay with her mother-in-law, Naomi, an older widow with no one left to care for her. Naomi had nothing to offer Ruth—no money, no home, no family connections. Yet, Ruth's loyalty was so deep that she willingly gave up her security to support Naomi and follow her into an uncertain future.

What makes this even more incredible is that Ruth didn't just follow Naomi out of a sense of duty. Her decision was an act of extraordinary faithfulness, love, and commitment. She embraced Naomi's people as her own and chose Naomi's God as her God. This kind of loyalty goes far beyond what most of us are used to; it's about putting someone else's needs above your own comfort or desires, even when the path ahead looks tough.

A New Start Full of Challenges and Surprises

When Ruth and Naomi arrived in Bethlehem, Ruth didn't just sit back. She got to work, gathering leftover grains in the fields so she and Naomi could eat. Ruth's hard work and kindness caught the attention of Boaz, a kind farmer who owned the fields. Impressed by Ruth's dedication to Naomi, Boaz made sure Ruth was safe and had plenty to

gather. Their story didn't stop there—Ruth's loyal-
ty and faithfulness led to her marriage to Boaz, and she became part of
the family line of King David and, eventually, Jesus!

Why Loyalty Rocks

Ruth's actions show us that true loyalty often requires sacrifice, stepping
into the unknown, and staying committed to those we care about, even
when things get tough. Sticking by your friends and family in difficult
times can lead to incredible, unexpected blessings and strengthen your
relationships in powerful ways. It's easy to enjoy the fun times, but loyalty
truly shines when you're there through life's hardest moments. This kind
of selfless loyalty is a powerful expression of love, done not for personal
gain but out of genuine care for others.

Let's Chat:

- Can you think of a time when you stuck by someone during a
  tough time? How did it make you feel?

- How can you show loyalty to your friends and family like Ruth was
  with Naomi?

Prayer:

Dear God, thank You for the beautiful example of Ruth, whose loyalty
shows us the power of faithfulness and commitment. Please help us to
develop that same kind of loyalty in our lives. Teach us to live with the
type of love, honor, and courage that Ruth showed, especially when it's
hard. In Jesus' name, Amen.

Fun Fact: The Ancient Practice of Gleaning

Woman Gleaning, Courtesy of Rijksmuseum, Europeana.

Did you know that the story of Ruth gives us a glimpse into the ancient practice of gleaning? Gleaning was a form of social welfare in ancient Israel, where farmers would leave the corners of their fields unharvested and allow the poor, widows, orphans, and foreigners to gather the leftover crops. This practice, seen in Ruth's time, wasn't just charity—it was a law! It showed how communities came together to care for their most vulnerable members.

Archaeological discoveries, including ancient farming tools, help us understand how important agriculture was during Ruth's time. These findings, along with the story of Ruth, give us a deeper understanding of how God's people worked together to support each other and follow God's commands to care for the needy.

Creative Corner

LOYALTY LINK

Discover the power of loyalty and teamwork through a fun, collaborative obstacle course!

MATERIALS:

- Rope, long scarf, or string
- Blindfolds (one per team)
- Household items for an obstacle course (chairs, pillows, cones)
- Timer

SET UP:

- Create a simple obstacle course in a safe area like your living room or backyard.
- Mark a clear start and finish line.

INSTRUCTIONS:

1. Form Teams: Split into two teams (or one if fewer than 4 participants). Each team holds onto a rope, symbolizing their commitment to stick together.

2. Blindfolded Guidance: One member of each team is blindfolded. While, the other team members guide the blindfolded player using only their voices and the rope.

3. Navigate the Course: Work together to get from start to finish, overcoming obstacles without letting go of the rope.

4. Role Reversal: After reaching the finish line, switch roles so everyone gets a turn being blindfolded.

QUESTIONS TO PONDER:

How did it feel to rely on each other?
Did you notice the importance of clear communication?
How does this game relate to everyday life?

Day 6

Daniel's Faithfulness

Scripture Spotlight:

"But Daniel purposed in his heart that he would not defile himself with the king's delicacies, nor with the wine which he drank. Therefore he requested of the prince of the eunuchs that he might not defile himself." - Daniel 1:8

Stepping into Daniel's Daring Journey

Welcome back as we step into another day of *Extraordinary Blessings to Ordinary People*. Today, we're focusing on the courageous life of Daniel, a man whose unwavering faith set the stage for divine interventions in the face of immense challenges.

A Test of Devotion

Daniel's journey begins in Daniel 1. When Daniel was taken to Babylon, he faced his first test. Surrounded by the king's luxurious feasts, Daniel chose to stick to a simple diet to avoid defiling himself with food that conflicted with his faith. His commitment to God's laws not only kept him physically healthy but also showed his loyalty to God, earning him favor and respect in a foreign land.

The Dream Interpreter

In Daniel 2, Daniel's wisdom truly shines when King Nebuchadnezzar needs someone to interpret his troubling dreams. Where others failed, Daniel succeeded. He explained that the dreams were messages from God, revealing His sovereignty (God's ultimate authority) over all nations and rulers—not just at that time but for all time to come. His ability to interpret these 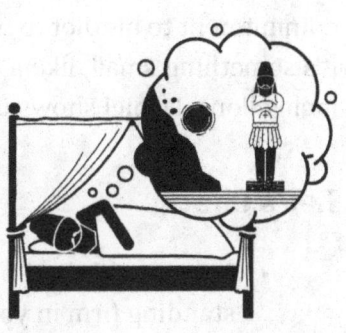 dreams lifted him to high positions within the kingdom, proving that his faith provided both integrity and valuable insights.

The Writing on the Wall

During King Belshazzar's reign, Daniel faced another significant challenge. In Daniel 5, a mysterious hand appeared at a royal feast and wrote on the palace wall. Once again, Daniel was called to interpret the message, which foretold the end of Belshazzar's reign. Fearlessly, Daniel proclaimed the truth, despite the risk of upsetting the king, showing his commitment to God's truth above human power.

Surviving the Lion's Den

Perhaps the most dramatic test of Daniel's faith came in Daniel 6 when he was thrown into the lion's den. Despite a decree that punished anyone who prayed to anyone other than the king, Daniel continued his daily prayers to God. Because of his faithfulness, God shut the mouths of the lions, and Daniel emerged unharmed, demonstrating that God protects those who remain faithful.

Faithful in All Things

Daniel's life teaches us about the power of consistent faith, from his commitment to his diet to trusting God more than fearing lions. Whether it's something small, like a decision about food, or life-threatening, like facing lions, Daniel shows us that God honors steadfast trust in Him.

Let's Chat:

- Can you think of a challenge you're facing today? What does "standing firm in your faith" look like in this situation?

- How can Daniel's faithfulness inspire you to stay strong in your faith?

Prayer:

Heavenly Father, thank You for the inspiring story of Daniel, who showed us how to be faithful in both small matters and great trials. Please help us face each day with faith, courage, and integrity, no matter what challenges we face. In Jesus' name, Amen.

Fun Fact: Daniel's Role in Ancient Empires

Neo-Babylonian Chronicle for years 605-594 BCE. British Museum. Image by Osama Shukir Muhammed Amin, CC BY-SA 4.0. Modified to black and white.

Did you know that Daniel's job as an advisor to kings wasn't just a biblical tale? His role aligns closely with documented historical positions in ancient Babylon and Persia. In these empires, advisors like Daniel were crucial to helping kings make decisions that impacted entire nations. Historical texts like the Babylonian Chronicles reveal that these advisors held significant power and responsibility—much like today's political advisors or cabinet members. They handled everything from legal matters to interpreting omens—yes, even dreams like Daniel's interpretations! These roles blended both administrative and spiritual duties, making them vital to the success of ancient governments. This shows that Daniel's work bridged the earthly and the divine, demonstrating how faith can shape the course of nations.

Creative Corner
DECODE LIKE DANIEL

Want to decipher and decode like a master detective? Get ready to start your epic adventure with a fun and interactive decoding game!

MATERIALS:

- Pens and paper for each participant
- Bibles for reference
- (For younger kids) Alphabet-to-number cipher sheets

CIPHER:

A = 1, B = 2, C = 3, D = 4, E = 5, F = 6, G = 7, H = 8, I = 9, J = 10, K = 11, L = 12, M = 13, N = 14, O = 15, P = 16, Q = 17, R = 18, S = 19, T = 20, U = 21, V = 22, W = 23, X = 24, Y = 25, Z = 26.

INSTRUCTIONS:

1. Inspiration Station: Think of words or short phrases that remind you of Daniel, like "brave," "wise," or "faithful."

2. Crafting Clues: For younger participants, write a number that correlates with the letter using the cipher above. For those up for a challenge, write a clue for each letter of your word using Bible verses. For example, the first letter of the third word in Daniel 2:20 = T.

3. Secret Exchange: Write your coded clues on a sheet and keep the chosen word a mystery. Then swap your secret code sheet with another participant and decode using your Bible or alphabet cipher to uncover the hidden word!

Day 7

Moses' Leadership

Scripture Spotlight:

"NOW THEREFORE GO, AND I WILL BE WITH YOUR MOUTH, AND TEACH YOU WHAT YOU SHALL SPEAK." - EXODUS 4:12

Stepping into the Shoes of a Leader

Welcome back as we wrap up our exciting journey through *Extraordinary Blessings to Ordinary People*. Today, we find ourselves standing at the shores of the Red Sea with Moses, a leader chosen by God to carry out one of the most daring and miraculous missions in history. From boldly confronting Pharaoh to guiding a nation through the wilderness, Moses' story is packed with jaw-dropping moments of courage, trust, and divine guidance.

The Call and Challenge

Moses' leadership journey started in a truly extraordinary way—a burning bush! As we read in Exodus 3, God called him to lead His people out of Egypt. A daunting task for anyone, let alone a shepherd who was once a prince, running away from Egypt because of his crime. Moses' hesitation and fear remind us that even the greatest leaders experience doubt (Exodus 4:10-13). But what made Moses special was that he didn't let his fear stop him. He trusted in God's power, and that trust led to a series of unforgettable miracles.

Parting the Red Sea

Picture this: Pharaoh's army is charging, the Israelites are panicking, and in front of them is nothing but endless water. It seemed like the end! But Moses, trusting in God's promise, raised his staff, and the impossible happened—the Red Sea parted (Exodus 14:21-31), creating a path to safety. This moment didn't just save the Israelites; it solidified Moses' role as a leader who trusted God fully, even when the odds seemed impossible.

Forty Years in the Wilderness

After crossing the sea, Moses' job was far from over. Leading the Israelites through the wilderness for forty long years was a massive test of patience and endurance. Moses had to deal with complaints, hunger, thirst, and moments of rebellion (Exodus 16-17, Numbers 11). Yet, he remained steadfast in his role, relying on God's guidance through it all. His journey teaches us that leadership often means staying strong when things are tough and trusting God to provide the way forward.

A Legacy of Law and Love

Perhaps Moses' greatest act as a leader came in Exodus 19-20, when he received and shared God's laws at Mount Sinai. These weren't just rules—they were the foundation for how God's people would live and grow together. Moses didn't just lead through action; he also led by teaching and guiding others to follow God's truth, shaping a nation that would continue to thrive under God's care.

Reflecting on Our Own Leadership

Moses' life shows us that leadership isn't about having all the answers or being the most confident person in the room. It's about trusting in God, facing challenges with courage, and guiding others with wisdom and compassion. Whether we're leading at home, in school, or in our communities, Moses' story encourages us to step up, knowing that God will be with us.

Let's Chat:

- Can you think of a time when you stepped up to lead others through a tough situation? What strengths did you discover about yourself?

- How does Moses' perseverance inspire you when you face challenges?

Prayer:

Lord, thank You for the inspiring example of Moses, who showed us how to lead with faith, courage, and humility. Please give us the strength to face our Red Seas, the wisdom to guide others, and the faith to trust in Your plans even when the journey is hard. Help us to lead by serving and to rely on Your guidance in every step we take. In Jesus' name, Amen.

Fun Fact: The Enigma of Mount Sinai

The peak of Jabal Maqla as seen from the plateau of the mountain. Image by Wikkiwooki, CC BY-SA 4.0.

Did you know that the exact location of Mount Sinai—where Moses received the Ten Commandments—is still one of the biggest mysteries of biblical archaeology? While many people think it's in the Sinai Peninsula in Egypt, some fascinating new theories suggest it could be in Saudi Arabia at a mountain called Jabal Maqla.

What makes Jabal Maqla so interesting is that its peak looks scorched, matching the Bible's description of God descending in fire and smoke (Exodus 19:18). Surrounding the mountain are vast plains that could have easily held the thousands of Israelites during their journey. Researchers exploring this area have uncovered ancient altars, inscriptions, and other clues that make this theory even more exciting.

Creative Corner

MOSES' MISSION GAME

Lead your "tribe" through the wilderness to the Promised Land by making smart decisions, working as a team, and experiencing a slice of biblical history!

MATERIALS:

- Large game board (drawn on cardboard or paper)
- Game pieces (small figures or tokens)
- Dice
- Paper or index cards to make Challenge and Blessing cards
- Optional: Crackers, bread, or cereal flakes to represent manna.

SET UP:

1. Draw the Game Board: Design a path from Egypt to the Promised Land with spaces for drawing challenge cards and obstacle spaces like "Parting the Red Sea," "Mount Sinai," and "Wilderness."
2. Create Challenge and Blessing Cards: Examples of Cards:
   - "Ten Commandments: Recite one Commandment to continue."
   - "Miriam's Dance: Lead your team in a quick dance to skip ahead one space."

GAME PLAY:

1. Start Your Journey: Players begin in Egypt and roll the dice to move along the path.
2. Face Challenges and Receive Blessings: When you land on a challenge or blessing space, draw a card and overcome the obstacle by answering trivia or performing a task, or receive a blessing.
3. Reach the Promised Land: The first player to navigate all the challenges and reach the Promised Land wins.

CHAPTER 6
THE UNDENIABLE BIBLE
&
APOLOGETICS

*Unraveling the Foundations of Our Faith and
Revealing Evidence to Support It.*

THE GREAT ISAIAH SCROLL

RANGE: 1300 - 1800
SOURCE: THE ISRAEL MUSEUM, JERUSALEM
WWW.IMJ.ORG.IL

Day 1

The Origins and Trustworthiness of the Bible

Scripture Spotlight:

"EVERY SCRIPTURE IS GOD-BREATHED AND PROFITABLE FOR TEACHING, FOR REPROOF, FOR CORRECTION, AND FOR INSTRUCTION IN RIGHTEOUSNESS,"- 2 TIMOTHY 3:16

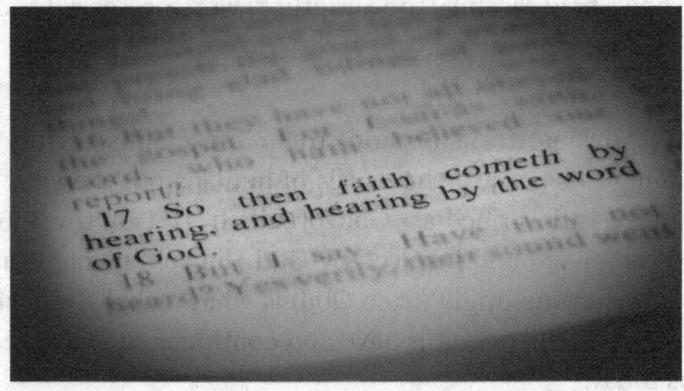

Exploring the Foundation of Our Faith

Welcome to the first day of our journey through *The Undeniable Bible and Apologetics*. Today, we unroll the scroll to explore the origins and trustworthiness of the Bible, the bedrock of our faith. How did the Bible come to us, and why can we trust it as a reliable source of truth? Let's uncover the answers together!

The Compilation of the Bible

The Bible isn't just one book—it's a collection of texts written by over 40 authors across three continents in three different languages over approximately 1,500 years. Despite these diverse backgrounds, the Bible presents a unified story about God's nature, human nature, and salvation. The process of determining which books were divinely inspired (from God) and included in the Bible was guided by strict criteria. Apostolic authorship, consistency with other Scriptures, and widespread acceptance among early Christians were all important factors in canonization.

Historical Manuscripts and Textual Integrity

The Bible's reliability is backed by more manuscript evidence than any other ancient document. The Dead Sea Scrolls, discovered in 1947, revealed some of the oldest known copies of the Old Testament, which match the medieval manuscripts we use today with incredible accuracy. This level of consistency, maintained over thousands of years, shows how carefully the Scriptures were preserved and copied.

Divine Inspiration

Beyond its physical transmission, the Bible claims divine inspiration—meaning it is not just the words of humans but the very Word of God. Scripture is described as "God-breathed" (2 Timothy 3:16), which means it was guided and inspired by God Himself, giving it authority and truth. This divine origin (from God) is what makes the Bible unlike any other book in history—it is alive and continues to guide, teach, and correct us today.

The Impact of Scripture

Throughout history, the Bible has shaped cultures, guided governments, and transformed countless lives. From ancient kings to modern leaders, people have turned to the Bible for wisdom, justice, and moral guidance. Its teachings have sparked revolutions, inspired humanitarian movements, and provided hope to individuals across the globe. What makes the Bible so powerful is not just its historical influence but its personal impact—it has the power to change hearts, renew minds, and transform lives. When we read Scripture, we encounter God's truth, and that truth has the ability to shape the world around us, as well as our own lives.

Reflecting on the Word

As we learned today, the Bible was written by many different authors in different languages and over many years, yet its message has stayed consistent and powerful. Its incredible influence on the world, as well as on individual lives, reminds us that the Bible truly is God's inspired Word. Understanding how the Bible came to be helps us appreciate it even more, and we can trust its teachings and promises.

Let's Chat:

- How does learning about the Bible's history and reliability affect your faith?

- How can knowing this help you trust Scripture more deeply as you read it?

Prayer:

Heavenly Father, thank You for giving us Your Word—a trustworthy and unchanging source of truth. As we learn about the origins and reliability of the Scriptures, please strengthen our faith and help us to cherish and live by Your teachings. In Jesus' name, Amen.

Fun Fact: Eyewitness Testimonies and the New Testament

 Did you know that much of the New Testament was written by eyewitnesses or those directly informed by them? For example, the Gospels of Matthew and John were written by two of Jesus' original disciples, who personally saw the events of His ministry, death, and resurrection. Luke, the author of the Gospel of Luke and Acts, was a close companion of Paul and carefully investigated the events he wrote about (Luke 1:1-4).

What's even more amazing is that the time between Jesus' life and the writing of the Gospels is remarkably short in historical terms. Most scholars agree that the Gospels were written within 40 to 60 years of Jesus' death, which is much closer than other historical accounts like the biographies of Alexander the Great, which were written over 400 years after his death. This proximity to the events helps ensure the accuracy and reliability of the Gospel accounts, making them not just religious texts but also valuable historical documents.

CREATIVE CORNER
Books of the Bible Mosaic

Create one artistic masterpiece from many pieces of art representing the one Bible made from all the books of the Bible!

Materials

- Paper
- Scissors
- Markers, colored pencils, or paints
- Large canvas, sturdy cardstock, or poster board
- Glue

Get Started:

1. <u>Prepare Pieces</u>: You'll need at least 66 pieces to represent each book of the Bible. Fold a sheet of paper in half, then again, and once more to create 8 sections. Cut these into strips, then cut each strip into 10 equal parts to make a total of 80 pieces.
2. <u>Decorate</u>: Each family member decorates pieces inspired by their favorite Bible stories, characters, or symbols.
3. <u>Visualize</u>: As a family, choose a simple yet meaningful image, like a cross, for your mosaic.
4. <u>Assemble</u>: Arrange the decorated pieces on the canvas to form the chosen image. Adjust as needed to achieve the perfect design.
5. <u>Glue each piece down</u>.
6. <u>Reflect</u>: Share the stories and inspirations behind your pieces. Each unique contribution adds to the overall impact and significance of the final masterpiece.

Enjoy this creative adventure together and marvel at your Bible-inspired mosaic!

Day 2

Archaeological Corroboration of the Bible

Scripture Spotlight:

"EVERY WORD OF GOD IS FLAWLESS. HE IS A SHIELD TO THOSE WHO TAKE REFUGE IN HIM." - PROVERBS 30:5

Exploring the Proof Beneath Our Feet

Welcome back to our journey through *The Undeniable Bible and Apologetics*. Today, we dig into the fascinating world of archaeology and how it confirms the historical events described in the Bible. Archaeologists have unearthed hundreds of artifacts that affirm the accuracy of the Bible's accounts. As we uncover just a few of these remarkable discoveries within the layers of history, we find tangible evidence that not only brings biblical stories to life but also deepens our connection to these ancient truths.

Unearthing Biblical Cities

Our adventure begins with the discovery of ancient cities mentioned in the Bible. Archaeologists have excavated sites like Jericho, where the walls famously fell as recorded in Joshua 6, and Hazor, mentioned in Joshua 11, which was defeated by the Israelites. These sites reveal layers of civilization and destruction that align with the biblical narrative, providing physical proof of the events described in Scripture.

Finding the House of David

One of the most significant archaeological finds is the Tel Dan Stele, a stone that mentions the "House of David" and confirms the existence of King David as a historical figure. This discovery is crucial because it supports the biblical account of David's royal lineage and the kingdom of Israel, linking biblical text with historical fact.

The Tel Dan Stele on temporary display at the Bible Lands Museum's Khirbet Qeiyafa exhibition. Image by Oren Rozen, CC BY-SA 4.0. Modified to black and white.

The Pool of Siloam

The Gospel of John describes Jesus healing a man born blind at the Pool of Siloam (John 9). For a long time, many thought this pool was symbolic or perhaps a myth—until archaeologists uncovered it in Jerusalem, exactly where John's Gospel said it would be. This discovery not only confirms the pool's existence but also adds historical weight to the Gospel account of Jesus' miracle.

Archaeology and the New Testament

Moving to the New Testament, archaeology gives us insight into the life and times of Jesus and the early Christians. For example, a fishing boat discovered in the Sea of Galilee dates back to Jesus' time, offering a glimpse into the lives of fishermen like Peter. Additionally, the ossuary (bone box) of Caiaphas, the high priest who presided over Jesus' trial, further links the Bible to history, confirming the accuracy of the biblical narrative.

Model of a fishing boat from the 1st Century BCE at the National Maritime Museum, Israel. Image by Deror avi, CC BY-SA 3.0. Modified to black and white.

Reflecting on the Evidence

Today's archaeological discoveries remind us that the Bible is not only a spiritual guide but also a reliable historical document. These finds echo the stories passed down through generations and give us confidence that the events described in the Bible truly happened.

Let's Chat:

- How does knowing about these archaeological discoveries enhance your faith in the Bible?

- What does it mean for your personal faith to know that the events described in the Bible are supported by historical evidence?

Prayer:

Lord, thank You for the gift of Your Word and the many ways You reveal its truth. Please help us to grow in our faith, strengthen our trust in You, and deepen our commitment to living out Your teachings. In Jesus' name, Amen.

Fun Fact: The Pilate Stone Reveals a Biblical Truth!

Holy Land 2016 P0230: Caesarea Maritima Pilate Stone. Image by Fallaner, CC BY-SA 4.0. Modified to black and white.

Imagine discovering a piece of history that confirms a major biblical figure's existence! That's exactly what happened in 1961 when archaeologists found the Pilate Stone in Caesarea Maritima, Israel. This stone slab bears an inscription that reads "Pontius Pilate, Prefect of Judea." It's a thrilling confirmation of the New Testament's account of the man who ordered Jesus' crucifixion. This artifact is like a direct link to the past, bringing the Bible's narrative to life in a whole new way. This incredible find not only solidifies Pilate's historical presence but also deepens our connection to the events of Jesus' final days.

CREATIVE CORNER

Design a Dig!

Get ready for an archaeological adventure! Whether you have a sandbox or just a simple container with sand, you can create your very own dig site right at home.

Materials Needed:

- Sandbox, large container, or garden section
- Salt dough or household items as artifacts
- Brushes, spoons, or small trowels for excavation

Setting Up Your Dig Site:

1. Bury Artifacts: Craft artifacts from salt dough or find small items to use as treasures. Bury them in your dig site.
2. Excavation: Use tools to carefully dig and uncover the hidden artifacts.

Salt Dough Recipe for DIY Artifacts:

Ingredients:

- 4 cups flour
- 1 cup salt
- 1.5 cups warm water

Instructions:

1. Mix Ingredients: Combine flour and salt in a large bowl. Gradually add warm water until the dough forms. Knead until smooth.
2. Shape Artifacts: Form the dough into shapes like coins, tablets, or pots. Add details with toothpicks.
3. Bake: Preheat oven to 250°F (120°C). Place artifacts on a parchment-lined baking sheet and bake for 2-3 hours, or until hard.
4. Decorate: Once cooled, paint your artifacts to resemble ancient finds.

Enjoy your archaeological adventure!

Day 3

Fulfilled Prophecies

Scripture Spotlight:

"Beginning from Moses and from all the prophets, he
explained to them in all the Scriptures the things
concerning himself." - Luke 24:27

Unraveling the Scrolls of Time

Welcome back to *The Undeniable Bible and Apologetics*! Today, we're unraveling the captivating world of fulfilled prophecies. The Bible isn't just a collection of ancient stories—it's a living book, full of prophecies written hundreds of years before they were fulfilled. These prophecies are like puzzle pieces that fit together to reveal a bigger, clearer picture of God's plan, perfectly fulfilled in Jesus Christ!

Prophetic Puzzles Becoming Clear Pictures

The Bible contains hundreds of prophecies that fore-told the coming of Jesus, the Messiah. These predic-tions weren't vague or general; they were specific and detailed. The fact that each prophecy was fulfilled so perfectly and precisely is one of the strongest proofs of the Bible's divine origin! Let's take a closer look at three major prophecies that were fulfilled in stunning ways by Jesus.

- **The Virgin Birth** – Imagine this: 700 years before Jesus was born, the prophet Isaiah boldly declared, "Behold, a virgin shall conceive and bear a son, and shall call his name Immanuel" (Isaiah 7:14). Now, while Jesus wasn't literally named "Immanuel," this prophecy was still powerfully fulfilled in Him! The name Im-manuel means "God with us," and that's exactly who Jesus is. In Matthew 1:22-23, the angel explains that Jesus' birth to Mary, a virgin, fulfills Isaiah's prophecy—Jesus is the ultimate expression of God with us! This isn't just a name—it's a promise that through Jesus, God would walk with us, teach us, and ultimately save us. Amazing, right?

- **The Suffering Servant** – Hundreds of years before Jesus was crucified, the prophet Isaiah gave a vivid and heart-wrenching description of someone who would suffer for the sins of others (Isaiah 53). This "Suffering Servant" would be rejected, beaten, and led like a lamb to the slaughter, yet by His wounds, we would be healed. Sound familiar? Jesus' life, death, and resurrection perfectly fulfill this prophecy! His sacrifice on the cross was not a tragic accident—it was part of God's plan all along, and Isaiah's words give us a glimpse of that plan in action. Through Jesus, the Suffering Servant, we are offered forgiveness and eternal life.

- **The Triumphal Entry** – Picture this: Zechariah, a prophet in the Old Testament, predicted that the Messiah would enter Jerusalem riding on a donkey—yep, a donkey! "Rejoice greatly, O daughter of Zion! Behold, your King is coming to you; He is just and having salvation, lowly and riding on a donkey" (Zechariah 9:9). Fast forward to Matthew 21:4-5, and we see Jesus riding into Jerusalem on a donkey, just as Zechariah had said. This wasn't just a random event—it was Jesus fulfilling a centuries-old prophecy, showing everyone that He is the humble yet victorious King who had come to save the world!

Living Proof: Prophecy Fulfilled

When we look at these fulfilled prophe-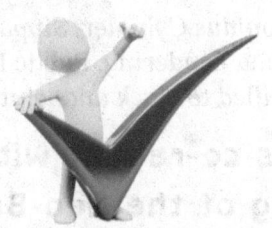
cies, we see something extraordinary:
God's promises never fail! The accuracy
of these prophecies is living proof that
God is in control, that His Word is true,
and that we can trust Him completely.
He's been faithful throughout history, and He'll be faithful in your life too!
These fulfilled prophecies remind us that God's plan is always unfolding,
even when we don't fully see it yet.

Let's Chat:

- How does understanding these fulfilled prophecies strengthen your faith?

- Can you think of ways God has fulfilled His promises in your own life or in the lives of those around you?

Prayer:

Heavenly Father, we are amazed by the accuracy and depth of Your Word, revealed through fulfilled prophecies. Please help us to trust in Your promises and Your timing. May our lives be a testament to Your faithfulness as we live out the reality of Your Word every day. In Jesus' name, Amen.

Fun Fact: Discovering a King's Name

Nabonidus Cylinder, Sippar. Photo by Jona Lendering, Public Domain. Modified to black and white.

Did you know that the Nabonidus Cylinders, ancient artifacts found in the ruins of Babylon, shed light on historical figures mentioned in the Bible? These cylinders mention Belshazzar, who was co-regent with his father Nabonidus, the last king of the Neo-Babylonian Empire. Before this discovery, some people doubted whether Belshazzar even existed! But this finding confirmed his role and supports the biblical narrative in the Book of Daniel. This is a great example of how archaeology continues to affirm the truth of the Scriptures, offering more insight into God's unfolding plan throughout history.

CREATIVE CORNER
Blueprint for a Helmet

As we explore how prophecies unfold and plans come to fruition, today's activity is all about creating blueprints for our own spiritual armor! Just like prophecies lay out God's plans, our helmet blueprints will prepare us for crafting real helmets next week. Let's design how our helmets should look, and get a taste of bringing a plan into reality!

Materials:

- Paper
- Pencils and erasers
- Colored markers, crayons, or paints
- Rulers for precise drawing

Instructions:

1. <u>Inspiration and Design</u>: Discuss how Bible prophecies laid out God's plans, which were fulfilled in remarkable ways. Creating a blueprint is like making a plan for your helmet, though unlike God's plans, ours may change. Look at different helmet designs—ancient warriors, sports helmets, fantasy helmets—for inspiration.
2. <u>Sketch Your Blueprint</u>: Draw your helmet design on paper, using your favorite stories or characters for inspiration. Be creative!
3. <u>Add Details</u>: Use rulers for straight lines and markers or paints for vibrant colors. Add special features like a symbolic crest or unique pattern.
4. <u>Share and Explain</u>: Once finished, share your designs and explain why you chose them.
5. <u>Prepare for Construction</u>: Place your blueprints in a visible spot to build anticipation for next week's crafting session.

Day 4

Consistency and Preservation of Scripture

Scripture Spotlight:

"YAHWEH, YOUR WORD IS SETTLED IN HEAVEN FOREVER." -
PSALM 119:89

Unrolling the Scroll of Time

As we continue our adventure through *The Undeniable Bible and Apologetics*, we unroll the ancient scrolls to explore the incredible consistency and preservation of the Bible over the ages. It's like tracing a message sent thousands of years ago and discovering it's still crystal clear today—no loss, no distortion, just truth preserved. How is that possible? Let's dig deeper.

Unchanging Message

The Bible's message has traveled through centuries, passed down by countless hands, yet it remains intact. This isn't just by chance—it's the result of God's providence and careful human effort. Take the Dead Sea Scrolls, for example. These ancient manuscripts, discovered in 1947, revealed that the Old Testament scriptures had been meticulously preserved for thousands of years with hardly any variation from what we read today. Imagine that! Ancient texts, copied by hand over centuries, and yet the message remains consistent. It's like finding an ancient treasure chest that holds exactly what we were promised.

The Role of Translation

Now, here's something that might blow your mind. The Bible has been translated into hundreds of languages, starting as far back as the 3rd century BC with the Greek Septuagint. And here's the amazing part: despite moving across cultures, time periods, and languages, the core meaning of the scriptures hasn't been lost. How is that possible? Scholars worked tirelessly, not just to "translate" words, but to carry over the full meaning, tone, and intent of the original texts.

It's like being given a map written in another language. If it were badly translated, you might get lost. But when scholars faithfully preserve the details, you can follow it with confidence. The translation process wasn't just about language; it was about ensuring that God's message could be understood by all people, in all times.

Modern Verification

 Today, with modern technology, we can compare ancient manuscripts to the versions of the Bible we read now, and guess what? The accuracy is astonishing! Whether it's the Dead Sea Scrolls or other ancient texts, scholars have found that the Bible remains consistent in its core messages and teachings. This isn't just proof of human diligence; it's a powerful reminder that God has watched over His word, making sure it remains a trustworthy guide for our lives.

Reflecting on Our Own Foundations

The fact that the Bible has been preserved so faithfully challenges us to think about how well we're preserving and living out the truths it teaches. Just as the scriptures have stood the test of time, we're called to stand firm in our faith, holding tightly to the truths God has entrusted to us.

Let's Chat:

- Knowing how the Bible has been carefully preserved and passed down, how does that impact your confidence in its teachings?

- How can you ensure that the truth of God's word continues to influence your life and the lives of those around you?

Prayer:

Heavenly Father, we are grateful for Your steadfastness in preserving Your word through the ages. Please help us to appreciate the depth of Your commitment to us, as shown through the careful transmission of the scriptures. Strengthen us to be faithful stewards of Your word, ensuring its message continues to guide us and future generations. In Jesus' name, Amen.

Fun Fact: The Incredible Materials of the Dead Sea Scrolls

Did you know that the Dead Sea Scrolls—one of the greatest archaeological finds of the 20th century—were written on a variety of materials? Most of these ancient texts were penned on parchment, made from specially prepared animal skins. Some were written on papyrus, a paper-like material made from the pith of the papyrus plant.

What's even more fascinating is how these materials survived for nearly two thousand years! Hidden in the caves near the Dead Sea, the dry climate helped preserve the scrolls. These ancient writings provide us with invaluable insights into the Bible's history and accuracy, giving us confidence that the scriptures we read today remain true to the original words of God.

CREATIVE CORNER
Handmade Paper

Materials:

- Scrap paper
- Water
- Blender
- Sieve/strainer
- Bowl
- Sponge
- Rolling pin/spoon
- Cloth/felt sheets

Instructions:

1. Tear the scrap paper into small pieces.
2. In a blender, cover the paper pieces with water and soak for a few hours. Then, blend until the mixture looks like thick pulp.
3. Pour the pulp mixture over a sieve or strainer placed over a bowl or sink to catch the water.
4. Spread the pulp evenly over a piece of cloth or a flat, porous surface.
5. Use a sponge to gently press down on the pulp to remove excess water, then flatten it into a thin sheet.
6. Let it dry completely (use sunlight to speed up the process).
7. Peel the paper off the cloth, and you have handmade paper!

Make a Scroll

Materials:

- Scrap Paper
- Sticks, chopsticks, or dowels
- String or ribbon
- Pencils

Instructions:

1. Prepare the Paper: Using a piece of paper, roll each end around a stick or dowel, and secure it with glue or tape.
2. Decorate: Decorate the paper with a favorite quote, a verse, or something inspirational.
3. Roll It Up: Once decorated, roll your paper around the dowels to form a scroll.
4. Tie It Up: Tie the scroll with string or ribbon to keep it close.

Day 5

The Credibility of the Disciples

Scripture Spotlight:

"For we didn't follow cunningly devised fables when we made known to you the power and coming of our Lord Jesus Christ, but we were eyewitnesses of his majesty." - 2 Peter 1:16

The Witness of the Witnesses:

Welcome back to another exciting day of *The Undeniable Bible and Apologetics*. Today, we're taking a closer look at the credibility of the disciples, whose firsthand accounts form the foundation of the New Testament. Unlike polished, flawless narratives, the Gospels offer a raw and unfiltered glimpse into their experiences—complete with discrepancies and unflattering moments. But rather than discrediting their testimony, these human details actually enhance their authenticity and make their accounts all the more reliable.

Eyewitness Accounts and Human Elements:

The disciples were ordinary men whose lives were transformed by their time with Jesus. Their writings reflect what they saw and experienced, not a harmonized, sanitized story. Differences in their accounts—like variations in the details of the resurrection appearances—demonstrate that they were independent witnesses rather than collaborators in a fabricated tale.

These variations make their testimony more believable, not less, as they mirror the way different people naturally recall the same events differently.

The Honesty of Hard Truths:

Interestingly, the Gospels include details that could be seen as embarrassing or detrimental to the cause of early Christians. For example, the disciples often misunderstand Jesus' teachings and fail him at critical moments, like Peter's denial of Christ or the disciples' fear and doubt even after seeing the resurrected Jesus. The inclusion of these honest moments argues against the disciples concocting a story; fabricators would likely portray themselves in a more heroic, flawless light.

Transformed Lives, Transformed World:

After Jesus' resurrection and ascension, the disciples—who had once been fearful and hiding—became bold proclaimers of the Gospel. They faced persecution and even death for their steadfast belief in what they had witnessed. They didn't gain worldly power or riches for their testimony; instead, they sacrificed everything, showing the incredible impact of what they had experienced. Their transformation from scared followers to world-changing leaders is powerful evidence of the truth of their testimony.

Reflecting on Our Own Beliefs:

The stories of the disciples invite us to think deeply about what shapes our own faith. Are we moved by superficial tales and simply following what we've heard, or are we building our beliefs on the real, life-changing truths that the disciples lived and witnessed? Their courage, struggles, and ultimate faithfulness remind us that true faith isn't just something we talk about—it's something we live out, even when it's hard.

Let's Chat:

- How do the differences in the disciples' accounts affect your understanding of the Gospels?

- Have you ever seen or experienced something so great that you couldn't wait to share it with others?

Prayer:

Lord, thank You for the testimonies of Your disciples, whose real experiences and transformations deepen our faith. Please help us to trust in their experiences and be inspired by their testimony. May we be open and willing to change for the greater good, just as they did. In Jesus' name, Amen.

Fun Fact: The Traveling Apostles!

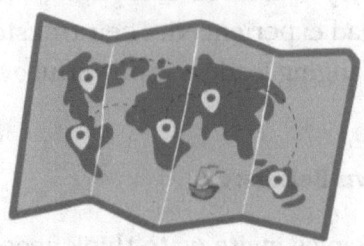

Did you know the apostles didn't stay local? They became fearless adventurers, traveling far and wide to spread Jesus' message to all nations, just as He commanded in Matthew 28:19.

For example, Thomas journeyed to India, leaving a legacy that lasts today. Paul traveled through Rome, Greece, and Turkey, spreading the Gospel and writing letters still read in churches. Andrew ventured to Scythia (modern-day Ukraine/Russia), while Peter preached in Rome, helping establish the early Christian church.

Thanks to their bold journeys and God's incredible love, we are privileged to know His Truth today and receive the gift of eternal life. Their faith took them across continents, transforming lives—including ours!

CREATIVE CORNER
Mapping Missions

Discover the paths taken by the disciples to spread Christianity, using a fun and educational map.

Materials:

- Large world map or globe
- Colored markers or pins
- Index cards (optional)

Instructions:

Prepare the Map or Globe:

- Place the world map on a wall or set the globe on a flat surface where everyone can see and reach it.
- Assign a different color marker or pin to each disciple, or just use your fingers to trace their journeys.

Mark the Routes:

- Start from Jerusalem and trace the routes each disciple took with your finger on the globe or map.
- If using a map, you can mark the routes with colored markers or pins, or simply discuss the routes as you point them out on the globe.

According to Eusebius (as cited by Christianity.com, n.d.), the Apostles spread out far and wide to preach the Gospel:

- Thomas journeyed to Parthia & India
- Andrew took the message to Scythia.
- John settled in Asia, later dying in Ephesus.
- Peter ministered in regions like Pontus, Galatia, Bithynia, Cappadocia, and Asia, before being martyred in Rome, where he requested to be crucified head-downwards.
- Paul preached from Jerusalem all the way to Illyricum and was martyred in Rome under Nero.

Discussion and Exploration:

- Have fun doing a little extra research and write down interesting facts about the locations or disciples.
- Talk about the cultural differences they may have encountered and how challenging it might have been to spread the good news.

Day 6

Historical Validation from Non-Christian Sources

Scripture Spotlight:

"ALTHOUGH I USED TO BE A BLASPHEMER, A PERSECUTOR, AND INSOLENT. HOWEVER, I OBTAINED MERCY BECAUSE I DID IT IGNORANTLY IN UNBELIEF." - 1 TIMOTHY 1:13

Tracing the Footsteps of History:

Welcome back to The Undeniable Bible and Apologetics. Today, we're tracing the footsteps of ancient historians who weren't Christians, but whose writings still validate key events and figures from the Bible. These historical accounts are like finding a hidden treasure, giving us incredible evidence that affirms the truth of the Scriptures!

Echoes from the Past:

When historians like Flavius Josephus, Tacitus, and Pliny the Younger documented their times, they weren't intending to support Christianity. They were simply recording historical facts as they understood them. Here are some amazing examples:

- **Flavius Josephus**, a Jewish historian, wrote about major figures from the New Testament, including John the Baptist and James. While scholars debate whether the James mentioned in his writings is Jesus' brother or another James, Josephus also references Jesus himself, describing Him as a wise teacher who performed extraordinary deeds and was crucified by Pontius Pilate. This gives us an independent mention of Jesus outside of Christian texts.

- **Tacitus**, a leading Roman historian, confirmed that Christ (called Christus) was executed under Pontius Pilate during the reign of Tiberius, placing Jesus' life and death within a historical timeline that aligns perfectly with the Gospels. Tacitus was not a fan of Christians, but his record of these events adds to their credibility.

- **Pliny the Younger**, a Roman governor, wrote about early Christians in his letters to Emperor Trajan, describing how they worshiped Christ as a deity and refused to renounce their faith—even in the face of death. His writings give us a clear picture of how committed and widespread the early Christian movement had become.

211

Why This Matters:

These historians had no agenda to promote Christianity. They were simply documenting events as they saw them. This gives their accounts even more value, as they unintentionally support what we read in the Bible. Their writings provide historical evidence that key figures and events from Scripture were real.

What does this mean for Our Faith Journey:

Discovering these historical confirmations is like uncovering ancient footprints leading us back to the truth of the Bible.

It shows us that our faith isn't based on fairy tales or legends—it's rooted in real events that were witnessed, recorded, and acknowledged even by those who didn't follow Jesus. These sources remind us that God's story isn't just something we read about in church—it's woven into the fabric of history itself! Knowing this strengthens our faith and gives us confidence that what we believe is both spiritually and historically true.

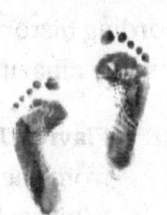

Let's Chat:

- How does learning about non-Christian historical sources that confirm biblical events impact your confidence in the Bible's accuracy?

- What does it mean for your faith when even those who didn't follow Jesus acknowledged Him in their historical records?

Prayer:

Lord, we thank You for the evidence that supports the truth of Your Word. Please guide us in using this knowledge to deepen our faith and to share Your message with boldness. In Jesus' name, Amen.

Fun Fact: The Power of Pliny's Letters!

Did you know that Pliny the Younger—a Roman governor around AD 112—wrote to Emperor Trajan asking how to deal with early Christians? He wasn't writing a history book but seeking advice on handling believers who refused to worship Roman gods. Pliny described how Christians would gather early to sing hymns to Christ "as to a god" and bind themselves by oath—not to commit crimes, but to live upright lives.

The beginning of Pliny's letters in the manuscript Cesena, Biblioteca Malatestiana, Ms. S.XX.2, fol. 1r. Public Domain. Modified to black and white.

This shows that even in the early 2nd century, Christians were already seen as a distinct group, worshiping Christ as divine. Pliny wasn't promoting their cause; he was trying to figure out how to manage them! His letter provides a valuable outsider's view of how deeply their faith impacted their lives.

Where to Read More: If you want to explore this and other ancient documents, you can find *The Antiquities of the Jews and The Jewish War* by Josephus, *The Annals* by Tacitus, and *Letters of Pliny* at Project Gutenberg's website: www.gutenberg.org

CREATIVE CORNER
Whodunit: Biblical Saviors Game

Solve the mystery of who saved the gentile, where it happened, and how it was done.

TOP SECRET

Get Ready to Play:

- Gather Your Detectives: Pick someone to be the game host. They will secretly choose the answers
- Secret Choices: The game host selects one name, one location, and one method from the lists below and writes them down. Hide the answers in an envelope or fold the paper to keep it secret.

WHERE:

Jerusalem
Rome
Babylon
Nineveh
the Red Sea

WHO:

Paul
Peter
Esther
Moses
Daniel

HOW:

A Miracle
Preaching
Testimony
Kindness
Facts

How to Play:

- Guess the Mystery: Each player takes turns guessing the name, location, and method.
- Clue Time: After each guess, the game host tells the player how many of their guesses were correct. Players should keep track and refine their next guess.
- The first detective to correctly guess the name, location, and method wins!

Have Fun!

Or make up your own names, locations, and methods to add a personal twist to the game!

Day 7

Unveiling the Universe's Blueprint

Scripture Spotlight:

"For the invisible things of him since the creation of the world are clearly seen, being perceived through the things that are made, even his everlasting power and divinity, that they may be without excuse." - Romans 1:20

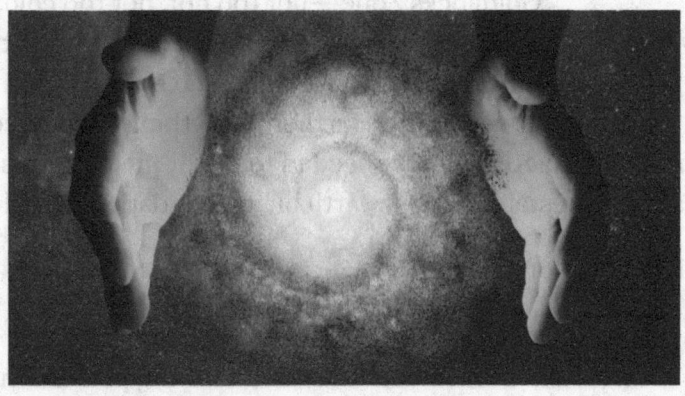

Sightseeing God's Remarkable Design:

As we wrap up *The Undeniable Bible and Apologetics*, we're going on a breathtaking sightseeing tour through God's creation! One of the clearest evidences of our great and loving God is all around us—we just have to stop and look. From the intricate details of the smallest molecule to the vastness of the universe, we are surrounded by undeniable evidence of His precision and craftsmanship. Whether you peer through a microscope or gaze into the night sky, everything points to the brilliance of our Creator. Let's explore a few of the incredible ways God's design is evident in the world around us!

Stars in Their Courses:

If we were to gaze up at the stars night after night, we'd see a predictable pattern. But did you know scientists believe the gravitational forces holding planets and stars in place are so finely tuned that even a slight shift could cause cosmic chaos? This perfect balance, which governs galaxies and solar systems, reminds us of Job 38:31, where God asks, "Can you bind the cluster of the Pleiades, or loosen the cords of Orion?" The stars themselves testify to God's flawless order in the universe.

The Perfect Spot for Life:

Earth is positioned in what scientists call the "Goldilocks Zone"—not too hot, not too cold, but just right for life to thrive. If we were even slightly closer to the sun, Earth would be too hot for liquid water. If we were a little farther, everything would freeze. God placed the Earth exactly where it needed to be for life to flourish, as the Psalmist says, "He established the earth on its foundations" (Psalm 104:5).

The Hidden Power of Trees:

When you look outside, you may see a tree—something we often take for granted. But trees are miraculous! They clean the air, provide fruit, shelter wildlife, and even produce medicine, like aspirin from willow bark.

Recently, scientists discovered that trees release essential oils called phytoncides, which have healing and stress-relieving effects on humans. This echoes the Bible's use of trees and leaves as symbols of healing and restoration, such as in Ezekiel 47:12, where the leaves of the trees by the river are described as being for healing. God designed them to be essential for our health and well-being!

The Miracle of DNA:

Now let's look even closer—to the human next to you. God created them in His image (Genesis 1:27), and while that's a deep truth, it also points to the complexity and uniqueness of the human body. Inside every cell of that  person is DNA—a tiny instruction manual. Scientists estimate that if all the DNA in one person were stretched out, it would reach the sun and back 600 times! Even more amazing, geneticists have discovered that all human DNA traces back to a common ancestor. No kidding—you mean like Adam and Eve? This microscopic code contains all the instructions needed to build and maintain our bodies. Psalm 139:13 says, "For you formed my inmost being. You knit me together in my mother's womb," showing us God's intentional involvement in our creation.

The Brain: A Marvel of Consciousness:

Even beyond the physical, our minds are an example of God's brilliant design. While computers excel at calculations, no machine can match the human brain's ability to think creatively, feel emotions, or understand right from wrong. Consciousness—the awareness of ourselves and the world around us—remains a mystery that science can't fully explain. Where does it come from? The Bible tells us that we were made in God's image, reflecting His ability to reason, create, and love.

What Does This Show Us?

Everywhere we look—from the tiniest molecule to the grandest galaxy—God's power, precision, and love are on display. These things aren't random; they're God's fingerprints on creation, telling the story of

His incredible design. We can trust that just as He designed the universe, He has a plan for each of us too.

Let's Chat:

- What amazes you most about God's creation?

- How does seeing God's precision affect how you trust Him in your daily life?

Prayer:

Heavenly Father, thank You for the wonders of Your creation that surround us every day. Help us to see Your hand in everything—from the smallest details to the vast universe. Strengthen our faith in Your perfect design, and let us live in awe of Your power and love. In Jesus' name, Amen.

Fun Fact: The Expanding Universe!

 Did you know that scientists discovered the universe is expanding like a balloon being blown up? This phenomenon, known as redshift, was first observed by studying distant galaxies. What's even more amazing is that the Bible hinted at this over 2,000 years ago! Isaiah 40:22 says God "stretches out the heavens like a curtain." This stretching of the universe aligns with modern discoveries, showing how science and God's Word beautifully intersect.

CREATIVE CORNER
Family Fingerprint Art

Turn your family's fingerprints into an amazing piece of art that shows off everyone's unique characteristics and how they come together to create something wonderful.

What You Need:

- Canvas, paper, or a poster board
- Ink pads or paints
- Cleaning supplies for fingers
- Optional: Picture frame

Steps:

1. <u>Plan Your Masterpiece</u>: Choose a theme together, like a garden of flowers, a galaxy of stars, or a tree with leaves. Each fingerprint will be part of this design.
2. <u>Set Up Your Space</u>: Protect surfaces with newspapers or an old cloth. Lay your canvas or poster board flat.
3. <u>Create Your Art</u>: Pick an ink pad or paint color, press your fingers on it, and then onto the canvas. Arrange prints for flowers, stars, or leaves. (Add details with markers or pens)
4. <u>Personalize It:</u> Write your name or initials next to your prints. Add a favorite quote or Bible verse.
5. Dry and Display: Let it dry completely. Hang it up!.
6. Reflect: Do you see how each person's fingerprints made the art special? Just like how everyone's unique characteristics strengthen and add to the beauty of your family.

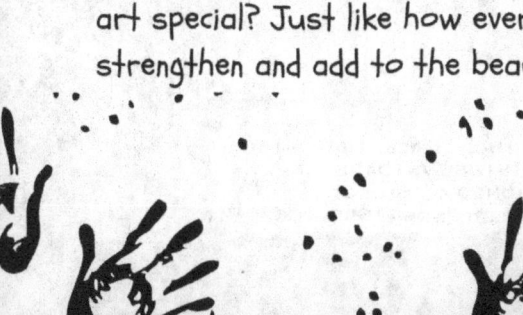

CHAPTER 7
ARMOR OF GOD
Equipping for Spiritual Battle

Quanto lacerà più
tanto più bella.

LA
POVERTA
CONTENTA
Descritta, e Dedicata
A'RICCHI
NON MAI CONTENTI
Dal P. Daniello Bartoli
Della Compagnia
di Giesu. 6.

Joan. Miele fecit.

Day 1

The Belt of Truth

Scripture Spotlight:

"STAND THEREFORE, HAVING THE UTILITY BELT OF TRUTH BUCKLED AROUND YOUR WAIST." - EPHESIANS 6:14

Arming Up

Welcome, warriors, to the final chapter of our journey: *The Armor of God!* Over the next seven days, we'll explore and create each piece of this spiritual armor, starting with the Belt of Truth. This vital piece of armor is like the belt of a Roman soldier—keeping all the gear secure and ready for action. In the same way, the Belt of Truth keeps us grounded and holds the rest of the Armor of God in place. It helps us stand firm in God's Word and prepares us for the battles we face.

Truth Ties

Our journey begins with understanding how important truth is to our faith and daily life.

- **God's Word is Truth:** The Bible is our ultimate source of truth, guiding us through life's challenges. Knowing and applying God's Word helps us see clearly what's right and wrong, just like a belt keeps everything together. Without it, things can easily fall apart.

- **Truth in Our Lives:** Living truthfully is more than just being honest; it means aligning our actions, attitudes, and decisions with God's principles. Whether it's standing up for what's right, admitting when we've made a mistake, or making choices that reflect God's truth, the Belt of Truth helps us live with integrity and avoid the traps of lies.

- **Truth in Action:** The Belt of Truth also gives us strength to stand firm against temptations and falsehoods. When we're rooted in God's truth, we're able to resist the lies of the world and the enemy, just as a belt keeps a soldier's armor secure. With the Belt of Truth, we're always ready for whatever comes our way.

Jesus and Truth

"JESUS THEREFORE SAID TO THOSE JEWS WHO HAD BELIEVED HIM, 'IF YOU REMAIN IN MY WORD, THEN YOU ARE TRULY MY DISCIPLES. YOU WILL KNOW THE TRUTH, AND THE TRUTH WILL MAKE YOU FREE.'" - JOHN 8:31-32

Wear Your Belt

As we begin each day, let's choose to strap on the Belt of Truth. Living, speaking, and following His truth sets us free from sin and deception. When we walk in God's truth, we can move forward confidently, knowing that we're protected and guided by Him.

Let's Chat:

- Can you think of a time when it was hard to tell the truth, like admitting a mistake?

- What are some ways you can live more truthfully and align your life with God's Word every day?

Prayer:

Heavenly Father, thank You for allowing us to know Your Word, which is our source of truth. Please help us to buckle on the Belt of Truth every day, guiding our lives to align with Your will. Strengthen us to stand firm against lies, temptations, and anything that pulls us away from Your truth. In Jesus' name, Amen.

Fun Fact: Buckle Up for Battle!

Did you know that in ancient Roman armor, the belt (known as the balteus or cingulum militare) wasn't just for holding up trousers? It was essential for securing other armor pieces and carrying weapons like the sword and dagger. The belt was often decorated with engraved plates and symbolized readiness and strength.

Just as a Roman soldier's belt was central to their preparation for battle, the Belt of Truth is vital for Christians to be spiritually prepared and protected. It holds all the other pieces of our armor in place and equips us to face life's challenges head-on!

CREATIVE CORNER

THE BELT OF TRUTH

This week, we're creating each piece of the Armor of God, starting with the Belt of Truth.

MATERIALS:

- Old belts or strips of sturdy cloth
- Markers
- Stickers

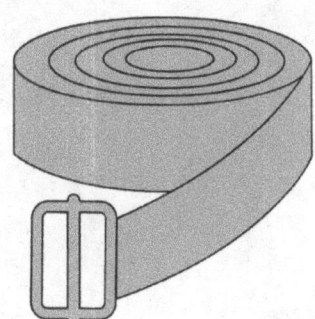

CRAFT:

- <u>Get Crafty</u>: Cut the cloth or use an old belt to fit around your waist.
- <u>Personalize</u>: Decorate your belt with markers and stickers. Write words or phrases that represent truth and honesty.
- <u>Wear Your Belt</u>: Let it remind you of the importance of living truthfully.
- <u>Discuss</u>: Talk about how being truthful builds trust in relationships and helps us follow God's guidance.

ALTERNATIVE ACTIVITY:

- <u>Draw a Character</u>: Start with a character drawing and add a belt.
- <u>Daily Add-Ons</u>: Every day in this Armor of God series, add a new piece of armor to your character.

Day 2

The Breastplate of Righteousness

Scripture Spotlight:

"STAND THEREFORE, HAVING THE UTILITY BELT OF TRUTH BUCKLED AROUND YOUR WAIST, AND HAVING PUT ON THE BREASTPLATE OF RIGHTEOUSNESS," - EPHESIANS 6:14

Additional Scripture Reflection:

"HE PUT ON RIGHTEOUSNESS AS A BREASTPLATE, AND A HEL-MET OF SALVATION ON HIS HEAD. HE PUT ON GARMENTS OF VENGEANCE FOR CLOTHING, AND WAS CLAD WITH ZEAL AS A MANTLE." - ISAIAH 59:17

Arming Up

Welcome to Day 2 of the *Armor of God* series. Today, we equip ourselves with the Breastplate of Righteousness, a vital piece of our spiritual armor. Just as a physical breastplate on a Roman soldier protects his heart and vital organs, the Breastplate of Righteousness shields our spiritual hearts and the core of who we are.

Righteousness Revealed:

So, what exactly is righteousness? Let's break it down:

- **God's Righteousness:** The Bible tells us that our own good deeds aren't enough to make us righteous before God. Imagine wearing a breastplate that's torn and dirty because of our sins. But Jesus changes everything: "For him who knew no sin he made to be sin on our behalf; so that in him we might become the righteousness of God." (2 Corinthians 5:21). This means Jesus gives us His perfect, clean, and strong breastplate to wear in spiritual battle.

- **Our Weakness:** Wearing this breastplate means admitting we aren't perfect, but God's strength shines through our weaknesses. We don't have to be strong on our own; we rely on Jesus' strength.

- **Righteous Living:** Wearing the breastplate isn't just for show. It's about choosing to live like the soldiers God made us to be. It's not about earning points; it's about making choices that align with God's will and reflect a changed heart. This protects us from bad influences and guides us in doing good.

What does Jesus say?

"BLESSED ARE THOSE WHO HUNGER AND THIRST AFTER RIGHTEOUSNESS, FOR THEY WILL BE FILLED." - MATTHEW 5:6.

Righteousness in Action

As we strap on the Breastplate of Righteousness, we're not just putting on a piece of armor; we're choosing to live out the character of Christ. This doesn't mean that we should pretend to have it all together or that we're perfect. Instead, we boldly admit our flaws and let God

work through our weaknesses. Each time we choose honesty, kindness, or patience, we show the power of righteousness in our lives, not through our strength but through His.

Let's Chat:

- How does knowing that our righteousness comes from Jesus change how you live every day?

- What can you do to make sure you wear the breastplate of righteousness daily?

Prayer:

Heavenly Father, thank You for the gift of righteousness through Jesus, which acts as a breastplate guarding our hearts. Please help us to wear it proudly and responsibly, living lives that reflect You. Please guide us in our actions and help us to stand firm against trials and challenges. In Jesus' name, Amen.

Fun Fact: A Breastplate for Every Battle!

Reconstruction of a Roman centurio, Museum Quintana - Roman department. Image by Wolfgang Sauber, CC BY-SA 3.0. Clipped to show the breastplate and modified to black and white.

Did you know that the Roman breastplate, known as the "lorica," came in various designs, each tailored for specific advantages? One popular type, the lorica segmentata, consisted of overlapping metal strips that provided both flexibility and strong protection, allowing soldiers to move freely while shielding their vital organs. Another type, the lorica squamata, featured scale-like metal plates, resembling fish scales, making it lighter and more comfortable for different combat situations. These versatile designs helped shield a soldier's heart and vital organs during battle. Just like these breastplates protected Roman soldiers, the Breastplate of Righteousness shields our hearts in spiritual warfare, helping us stand strong and resist the enemy's attacks!

CREATIVE CORNER

THE BREASTPLATE OF RIGHTEOUSNESS

MATERIALS:
- Large paper bags or paper
- Scissors
- Paint, markers, or crayons
- Staples, glue, or tape

CRAFT:

Choose Your Material:
- If using a paper bag: Cut a hole in the bottom of the bag for your head. Then, cut the sides straight down almost to the bottom, leaving a couple of inches for your shoulders.
- If using construction paper, use one piece for the front and one for the back of your breastplate.

Assemble Your Armor: Staple, glue, or tape paper strips or string from one side to the other to create shoulder straps and connect the sides, leaving room to easily pull your breastplate off and on.

Get Creative: Use your imagination to decorate your breastplate with paint, markers, and stickers. Aluminum foil also works great for a shiny look!

Suit Up: Wear your breastplate as a powerful reminder of how living righteously protects you.

ALTERNATIVE ACTIVITY:

Draw Your Armor: Add a breastplate to your character drawing from Day 1.

REMEMBER, THIS IS JUST A GUIDE TO GET YOU STARTED. USE YOUR CREATIVITY AND MAKE IT AS UNIQUE AS YOU ARE!

Day 3

The Shoes of the Gospel of Peace

Scripture Spotlight:

"STAND THEREFORE... HAVING FITTED YOUR FEET WITH THE PREPARATION OF THE GOOD NEWS OF PEACE." - EPHESIANS 6:15

Additional Scripture Reflection:

"HOW BEAUTIFUL ON THE MOUNTAINS ARE THE FEET OF HIM WHO BRINGS GOOD NEWS, WHO PUBLISHES PEACE, WHO BRINGS GOOD NEWS, WHO PROCLAIMS SALVATION, WHO SAYS TO ZION, 'YOUR GOD REIGNS!'" - ISAIAH 52:7

Arming Up

Welcome back to the Armor of God series! Today, we're lacing up the Shoes of the Gospel of Peace, an essential piece of our spiritual armor. Just as sturdy shoes protect a soldier's feet from blisters and rocky roads, these spiritual shoes give us firm footing to walk confidently in our faith and share the Good News with the world. So, grab your best spiritual sneakers, and let's get going!

Walking in Peace

Our journey today explores how the Shoes of the Gospel of Peace guide our steps:

- **Gospel Readiness:** The Shoes of the Gospel of Peace remind us to always be prepared to share the Good News of Jesus Christ. And it's not just about words—it's how we live! When others see the difference Christ makes in our lives, we are like a walking advertisement for the true stability and joy that comes from knowing Him.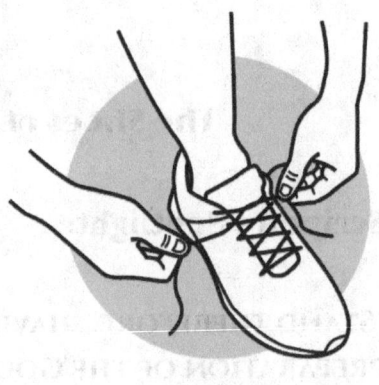

- **Walking in Peace:** These shoes aren't just for show—they're built to last! With them, we carry the peace of Christ with us wherever we go. And here's the kicker: these shoes aren't just for easy strolls in the park; they're all-terrain and meant to last through tough situations and uphill battles. They help us to stand firm against all kinds of spiritual attacks.

- **Spreading Peace:** These shoes are also built for distance. When we walk in peace, we're spreading Christ's love to everyone around us. Every step you take is an opportunity to show someone kindness, spread joy, and encourage others. Our actions can have a lasting effect, like leaving little footprints of the Gospel behind. With good shoes, we are capable of going far and wide, spreading the Good News just as the apostles did.

What does Jesus say?

"BLESSED ARE THE PEACEMAKERS, FOR THEY SHALL BE CALLED CHILDREN OF GOD." - MATTHEW 5:9

The Peacemaker's Path

Jesus encourages us to be peacemakers, not just through our words but in how we live, interact, and treat others, living out the Gospel of Peace and sharing it with those around us.

Let's Chat:

- How can we share the peace of Christ with others in our daily lives?

- What are some ways to be peacemakers in our relationships, both at home and outside?

Prayer:

Lord, thank You for the Shoes of the Gospel of Peace, which give us firm footing in our journey with You. Please help us to walk in peace, living out and sharing the Good News with others. Guide us to be peacemakers in our families, friendships, and communities, reflecting Your love and grace. In Jesus' name, Amen.

Fun Fact: Striding Strong!

Did you know that Roman soldiers' shoes, called caligae, were considered some of the best footwear of their time? These weren't your typical sandals—caligae had thick leather soles embedded with metal studs, almost like modern cleats. The metal studs

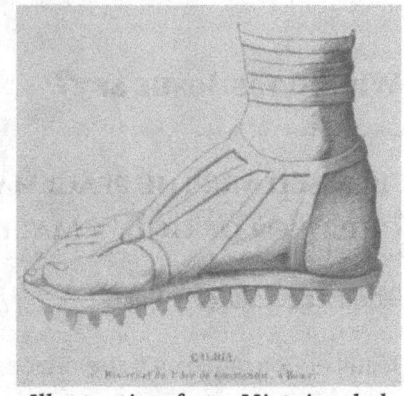

Illustration from Histoire de la chaussure by Ferdinand Seré (1818–1855). Public Domain.

provided incredible grip on rough or slippery terrain, making it easier for soldiers to keep their balance on long, grueling marches. Plus, the open design allowed for ventilation, which helped keep their feet cool and prevented blisters on hot days. For a Roman soldier, these sturdy sandals were essential gear, giving them the stability and durability they needed for battle and long-distance travel.

Just like Roman soldiers needed top-notch footwear to be effective in combat, we need the Shoes of the Gospel of Peace to support us as we carry the message of Christ wherever we go!

CREATIVE CORNER
THE SHOES OF THE GOSPEL OF PEACE

MATERIALS:

- Cardboard
- Plastic, paper, leather, old clothes, or any other flexible material
- Glue, staples, or a needle and thread
- Markers, paint, or crayons
- Hole punch
- Optional: Shoelaces or string

CRAFT:

1. <u>Trace and Cut</u>: Trace your feet on the cardboard, leaving room for your toes to wiggle. Cut out the shapes to create your shoes.
2. <u>Design Your Shoes</u>: Choose material for the shoe uppers. Wrap it around your feet and the cardboard soles to determine size and shape.
3. <u>Attach the Uppers</u>: Securely attach the soles to the flexible material using glue, staples, or needle and thread.
4. <u>Add Laces</u>: Punch holes along the edges and thread shoelaces through. Or, create a slip-on design.
5. Decorate: Add designs or decorations that remind you of the Gospel of Peace.
6. <u>Wear your shoes</u>: Wear them as a symbol of spreading the Gospel of Peace.

ALTERNATIVE ACTIVITY:

Draw shoes on your character in the Armor of God drawing.

Day 4

The Shield of Faith

Scripture Spotlight:

"ABOVE ALL, TAKING UP THE SHIELD OF FAITH, WITH WHICH YOU WILL BE ABLE TO QUENCH ALL THE FLAMING DARTS OF THE EVIL ONE." - EPHESIANS 6:16

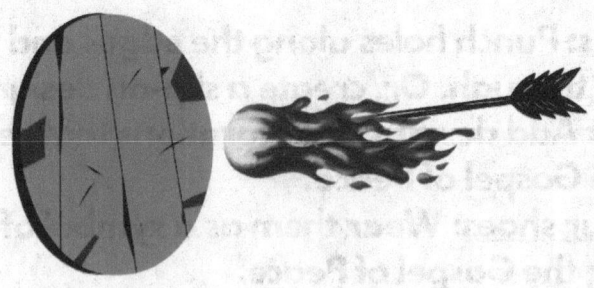

Arming Up

Welcome to Day 4 of the *Armor of God* series! Today, we take up the Shield of Faith, another essential piece of our spiritual armor. In ancient battles, a shield wasn't just an accessory—it was a lifesaver, deflecting arrows and blocking blows. In the same way, our faith acts as a shield, protecting us from doubts, temptations, and spiritual attacks.

Fortifying Faith

Let's explore the incredible protective power of faith:

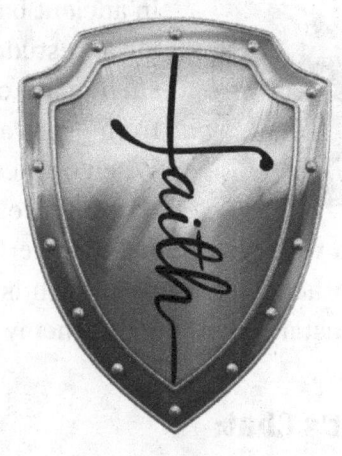

- **Deflecting Doubts:** In battles—and in life—it's easy to doubt when we can't see the full picture or understand the plan. But by holding up the Shield of Faith, we're saying, "Alright, God, I might not know what You know or see what You see, but I'll trust You today." Just like a sturdy shield protects a soldier, our faith allows us to deflect or brush off the arrows of doubt and fear. This shield isn't just for times when life is easy; it's about trusting that God's plan is best, even when things feel tough or uncertain.

- **Extinguishing Attacks:** Ancient shields were often soaked in water so they could extinguish flaming arrows on impact. If left dry, however, these wooden shields could burn up, leaving soldiers vulnerable. Like those shields, we must stay "soaked" in our faith, constantly refreshed by the Word, so that any flaming arrows of the enemy—thoughts of despair, temptations, or attacks on our hope—are immediately extinguished. When we notice these "flaming arrows" in our minds, it's time to drench ourselves in God's Word to stay protected.

- **Steadfast Assurance:** With the Shield of Faith, no words meant to discredit, deceive, or discourage us can shake us. Like a shield that bounces off every blow, we stand strong against the lies that may come our way. We know the truth, and we hold tight to it! Our faith isn't based on passing opinions but on the timeless truths of Scripture and the unchanging character of God. Holding this shield means we're rooted in what we know of God from His Word, remaining steadfast no matter what comes.

Ancient Warfare Tactics

 In ancient battles, soldiers would huddle close, forming a "testudo" or tortoise formation—like a protective shell made of shields. This formation covered them from every angle, even when they were surrounded. When we face attacks from all sides, we can strengthen our defense by standing together in faith. United in this way, we become a powerful force, supporting and protecting one another. This unity in faith is our greatest strength, equipping us to withstand anything the enemy tries to throw our way.

Let's Chat:

- How has faith protected you in difficult times?

- What are some ways you can strengthen your faith to better defend against spiritual challenges?

Prayer:

Lord, thank You for the Shield of Faith, which offers us protection against the assaults of the enemy. Please strengthen our faith daily, so that we may stand firm and extinguish all the flaming arrows aimed at us. May our trust in You grow stronger with each challenge we face. In Jesus' name, Amen.

Fun Fact: Full-Body Protection!

Did you know that Roman soldiers carried large, curved shields called "scutum"? These weren't just ordinary shields! Standing about as tall as the soldier himself, the scutum was crafted from wood, layered with leather, and reinforced with metal edges. This construction made it light enough to carry in battle but tough enough to with-

Reconstruction of an Antique Roman Scutum

stand fierce blows. The curve of the shield helped deflect attacks from every direction, giving the soldier greater protection than a flat shield would. The scutum was so well designed that it was a key reason for the Roman army's success. Just like this mighty shield, our Shield of Faith is meant to be our trusted protector, allowing us to face whatever comes our way with confidence!

CREATIVE CORNER
THE SHIELD OF FAITH

MATERIALS:
- Large cardboard
- Paint
- Glue
- Decorative materials (foil, fabric, etc.)

CRAFT:

1. **Cut Out Your Shield:**
- Cut your cardboard into a unique shield shape.
2. **Get Creative:**
- Paint and decorate your shield with bold colors, symbols that represent faith, or add foil for a shiny effect.
3. **Suit Up:**
- Carry your shield and discuss what it protects you from.

ALTERNATIVE ACTIVITY:

Draw Your Armor: Add an awesome shield to your character in the Armor of God drawing. Make it as detailed and unique as possible.

Day 5

The Helmet of Salvation

Scripture Spotlight:

"TAKE THE HELMET OF SALVATION..." - EPHESIANS 6:17

Additional Scripture Reflection:

"HE PUT ON RIGHTEOUSNESS AS A BREASTPLATE, AND A HEL-
MET OF SALVATION ON HIS HEAD. HE PUT ON GARMENTS OF
VENGEANCE FOR CLOTHING, AND WAS CLAD WITH ZEAL AS A
MANTLE." - ISAIAH 59:17

Arming Up

Welcome back, warriors, to another thrilling day of the *Armor of God* series! Today, we put on the Helmet of Salvation, a fundamental piece of our spiritual armor. Think of a helmet not just as a piece of metal for protection but as essential gear that ensures a soldier's survival in battle. Similarly, the Helmet of Salvation is vital for our spiritual survival and can protect our minds from attacks like intrusive thoughts of doubt, fear, or despair.

Understanding Salvation

Salvation is more than just a theological term—it's the very core of our life and hope in Christ:

- **What is Salvation?** Salvation is God's rescue from the consequences of our sins—spiritual death. Because of Jesus' death and resurrection, we are saved from sin's penalty and given the promise of eternal life with God. Romans 6:23 explains, "For the wages of sin is death, but the free gift of God is eternal life in Christ Jesus our Lord." Salvation restores our relationship with God, allowing us to live forever with Him.

- **Why is it Important?** Without salvation, we owe a debt for our sins that we can never repay on our own. But God, in His mercy, freed us from this debt through Jesus' sacrifice. The Helmet of Salvation is our reminder that the price has been paid in full. When doubts arise about God's love or our worth, this helmet reminds us of our true identity: redeemed, restored, and valued members of God's family.

- **Living in Light of Salvation:** With this helmet, we have the confidence to stand firm, knowing that nothing can separate us from God's love (Romans 8:38-39). This truth changes everything about how we live. It fills us with hope and gives us courage to face life's battles. When we wear this helmet, we carry the assurance that we are protected, loved, and destined for eternal life with God.

What else does Scripture say?

"THEREFORE, IF ANYONE IS IN CHRIST, HE IS A NEW CREATION; THE OLD HAS GONE, THE NEW HAS COME!" - 2 CORINTHIANS 5:17

"FOR WITH THE HEART ONE BELIEVES, RESULTING IN RIGHTEOUSNESS, AND WITH THE MOUTH, CONFESSION IS MADE, RESULTING IN SALVATION." - ROMANS 10:10

"HE PUT ON RIGHTEOUSNESS AS A BREASTPLATE, AND A HELMET OF SALVATION ON HIS HEAD. HE PUT ON GARMENTS OF VENGEANCE FOR CLOTHING, AND WAS CLAD WITH ZEAL AS A MANTLE." - ISAIAH 59:17

"RECEIVING THE RESULT OF YOUR FAITH, THE SALVATION OF YOUR SOULS. CONCERNING THIS SALVATION, THE PROPHETS SOUGHT AND SEARCHED DILIGENTLY. THEY PROPHESIED OF THE GRACE THAT WOULD COME TO YOU," - 1 PETER 1:9-10

These passages illustrate the gift and importance of salvation—how putting on our helmets allows us to confidently know that nothing can shake our knowledge of God's saving power, our Savior, and our eternal life.

Let's Chat:

- How has understanding your salvation shaped the way you handle life's challenges?

- What can you do to constantly remind yourself of the salvation you have in Christ?

Prayer:

Heavenly Father, thank You for saving us and for teaching us about the Helmet of Salvation. Please help us put on this helmet each day—not only to protect our minds but also to remind us constantly of the great sacrifice Jesus made for us. Strengthen us to live in the light of this truth, confident in our identity as Your saved and beloved children. May we shine Your light brightly in a dark world. In Jesus' name, Amen.

Fun Fact: A Helmet Fit for Battle!

Did you know that ancient helmets often featured intricate designs and were crafted to reflect the rank and achievements of the wearer? Roman helmets, known as galea, had unique crests and symbols that distinguished soldiers on the battlefield. Just as these helmets marked soldiers' identities and roles, the Helmet of Salvation marks us as children of God, loved and saved, with victory over spiritual enemies. This helmet is more than armor—it's a symbol of our identity and assurance in Christ.

CREATIVE CORNER

THE HELMET OF SALVATION

Remember the blueprint you made last week?
It's time to follow your pattern and instructions!

CRAFT: Use construction paper, cardboard, aluminum foil, or any material you like to create your helmet. Decorate it to match your ideas.

OR, MAKE A PAPER MACHE HELMET:

(for those with a couple of days and who don't mind a mess)

Materials: Balloon, newspaper, white glue or flour and water, paint, decorative items like feathers.

Steps:

1. Inflate a balloon to fit your head as a mold.
2. Tear newspaper into around 2" strips.
3. Mix white glue with water or mix flour and water to create a paste.
4. Dip newspaper strips in the paste, squeeze off excess, and layer them over the balloon. Cover with several layers, leaving an opening at the bottom for your head.
5. Let it dry completely (about a day or two).
6. Pop the balloon and remove fragments.
7. Paint and decorate your helmet to symbolize the protection and beauty of salvation.

ALTERNATIVE ACTIVITY:
Add a helmet to your Armor of God drawing.

Day 6

The Sword of the Spirit

Scripture Spotlight:

"AND TAKE THE SWORD OF THE SPIRIT, WHICH IS THE WORD OF GOD." - EPHESIANS 6:17

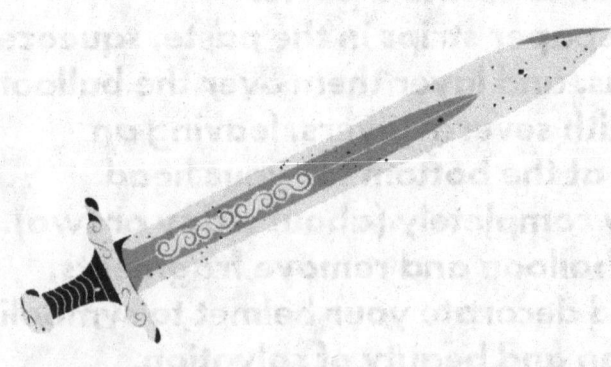

Arming Up

Welcome to Day 6 of the *Armor of God* series! Today, we equip ourselves with the Sword of the Spirit, the Word of God. Unlike the other pieces of armor that protect us, this sword is our powerful offensive weapon, helping us actively fight against lies, temptations, and anything that tries to pull us away from God.

Wielding the Word

 Just like a skilled warrior practices with their weapon, we must know and understand God's Word to use it effectively. Let's explore how we can make it an active part of our spiritual armor.

- **Why the Word?** The Bible tells us that God's Word is alive and powerful, sharper than any two-edged sword (Hebrews 4:12). It cuts through confusion, reveals truth, and helps us see what's really going on in our hearts. This makes it an essential tool for making wise choices and standing strong in spiritual battles.

- **Using the Sword:** To use the Sword of the Spirit effectively, we must know it well. This means regularly reading, meditating on, and applying God's Word. The more familiar we are with Scripture, the better equipped we'll be to use it in times of need. Jesus showed us how to do this by quoting Scripture when tempted by Satan, challenged by religious leaders, and even during His last moments on the cross. He used the Word as His ultimate weapon.

- **Defending and Attacking:** The Sword of the Spirit helps us both defend against spiritual attacks and boldly take action to spread God's truth. We use it to speak the truth, cut through lies, and share God's love and truth with others.

What does Scripture say?

"FOR THE WORD OF GOD IS LIV-
ING AND ACTIVE AND SHARP-
ER THAN ANY TWO-EDGED
SWORD, PIERCING EVEN TO
THE DIVISION OF SOUL AND
SPIRIT, OF JOINTS AND MAR-
ROW, AND IS A DISCERNER OF
THE THOUGHTS AND INTENTS
OF THE HEART." - HEBREWS 4:12

"IN HIS RIGHT HAND HE HELD
SEVEN STARS. OUT OF HIS
MOUTH PROCEEDED A SHARP
TWO-EDGED SWORD. HIS FACE
WAS LIKE THE SUN SHINING AT
ITS BRIGHTEST." - REVELATION 1:16

These verses illustrate the power and activity of God's Word, like a sword that not only protects but also helps us fight our spiritual battles.

Let's Chat:

- How have you experienced the power of God's Word in your life?
- What can you do to better equip yourself with the Sword of the Spirit?

Prayer:

Heavenly Father, thank You for giving us the Sword of the Spirit, Your holy Word. Help us to dive deep into Scripture, not only to defend against evil but also to spread Your truth boldly. Equip us to study diligently and use Your Word to make a positive impact in the world for Your glory. In Jesus' name, Amen.

Fun Fact: Sharpening Up!

Did you know that Roman soldiers would spend hours, nearly every day, sharpening, cleaning, and honing their swords to perfection? For them, a dull blade wasn't just ineffective—it could mean the difference between life and death in battle. In the same way, we need to keep our spiritual sword—the Bible—sharp and ready. By continually honing our knowledge of God's Word, we strengthen our understanding, refine our hearts, and prepare ourselves to stand firm against any challenges that come our way. With truth engraved in our hearts and God's strength by our side, we're fully equipped to face every battle confidently.

CREATIVE CORNER

THE SWORD OF THE SPIRIT

MATERIALS:
- Cardboard
- Aluminum foil
- Tape
- Markers, paint, or crayons

CRAFT:
1. <u>Cut</u>: Start by cutting out a fierce sword shape from the cardboard. Imagine you're crafting a mighty weapon!
2. <u>Wrap</u>: Wrap the blade in shiny aluminum foil to give it that authentic, metallic look.
3. <u>Handle</u>: Use tape to create a sturdy handle. Make it grip-worthy for epic battles!
4. <u>Decorate</u>: Now, let your creativity shine! Decorate the handle and write your favorite scripture to make your sword truly unique.
5. <u>Suit Up</u>: Imagine wielding this mighty sword in your spiritual battles.

ALTERNATIVE ACTIVITY:
Add a sword to your character in the Armor of God drawing

Day 7

Prayer

Scripture Spotlight:

"WITH ALL PRAYER AND REQUESTS, PRAYING AT ALL TIMES IN THE SPIRIT, AND BEING WATCHFUL TO THIS END IN ALL PER-SEVERANCE AND REQUESTS FOR ALL THE SAINTS." - EPHESIANS 6:18

Arming Up

Welcome, warriors, to our final day of the Armor of God series! Today, we focus on Praying in the Spirit, the action that fuels and completes our spiritual armor. This isn't just the end of a chapter; it's a commitment we carry forward beyond this book—through every season, every victory, and every challenge.

Prayer Warrior

Continuous prayer is like staying connected to a command center. By keeping in close contact with God, we move confidently through life's battles, knowing that while we may not see every obstacle ahead, He does. God guides, warns us of danger, and sends us help exactly when we need it. Let's explore what it means to pray like a warrior:

- **Prayer as Our Lifeline:** Prayer isn't just a powerful weapon—it's our lifeline to God. It's a gift, a time set apart to deepen our relationship with Him, making our bond with God unbreakable. Whether we're offering praise, gratitude, confession, or seeking guidance, prayer keeps us connected, open, and ready for God to work in our lives.

- **Conversations with God:** While building a habit of prayer is essential, true prayer is personal and sincere. Jesus taught us that it's not about impressing others but about having genuine moments with God. "But you, when you pray, enter into your inner room, and having shut your door, pray to your Father who is in secret; and your Father who sees in secret will reward you openly." - Matthew 6:6. Prayer is our opportunity to speak openly and privately with our Heavenly Father.

- **How to Pray:** Ever felt lost for words? When the disciples asked, "Teach us to pray," Jesus gave them what we now call the Lord's Prayer (Matthew 6:9-13). This powerful prayer is our guide when we're unsure how to start. And when life's battles leave us heartbroken, overwhelmed, or silent, the Holy Spirit steps in to pray with and for us. Romans 8:26 reminds us that when we don't know what to say, "the Spirit himself makes intercession for us with groanings which can't be uttered." So even when we're speechless, prayer is still the answer!

Staying Unified in Prayer

In battle, soldiers stay connected on a shared radio channel, all tuned to the command center and to each other. This unified connection keeps them informed, secure, and in sync. Similarly, when we pray together, it's like joining that same channel, linking us not only to each other but directly to God. Jesus said, "For where two or three are gathered together in my name, there I am in their midst." - Matthew 18:20. And even when we can't pray together, it's important to pray for one another. Just as Paul encouraged the Ephesians to lift him up in prayer: "Pray in the Spirit at all times with all kinds of prayers and requests. With this in mind, be alert and always keep on praying for all the saints." - Ephesians 6:18. So, let's suit up and fight in the unseen battle for our teammates, praying wholeheartedly for each other's strength and victory in Christ!

Let's Chat:

- When is your favorite time to pray?
- Who is someone you feel led to pray for right now, and how might you lift them up in prayer?

Prayer:

Heavenly Father, thank You for the gift of prayer and for the Holy Spirit, who helps us to pray. Please guide us to live with this armor on every day, strengthened by our commitment to prayer. May we be the warriors You intended us to be, seeking Your will, ready to lift others up, and growing deeper in our relationship with You. In Jesus' name, Amen.

Fun Fact: Prayer Powerhouse!

Catacomb in Rabat, Malta

Did you know that early Christians often gathered in catacombs and remote places to pray, especially during times of persecution? They would use the Psalms as their prayer books, turning these underground spaces into powerful centers of worship and faith. The Psalms provided words when they needed them most, linking their hearts to God's promises and strengthening them to persevere. Praying Scripture remains a powerful practice to this day, helping us align our prayers with God's will and connect with a faith that has stood strong for centuries!

On another note, have you ever wondered why we often pray with hands clasped together or lifted high? Studies show that physical gestures can signal our brains to pay attention. When done regularly, these prayer postures may help reduce distractions and keep us calm and focused. So, whether you pray with your hands held high or clasped together, your body knows it's time to shut down the distractions and concentrate!

CREATIVE CORNER
PRAYER

As we finish the Armor of God series, let's arm ourselves with prayer. Remembering what we've learned and commit to putting on the full Armor of God every day. Stay strong and ready for any battle.

MATERIALS:

- Comfortable pillows
- A quiet spot

ACTIVITY:

1. Find Your Spot: Pick a peaceful area in your home.
2. Set Up: Arrange comfortable pillows to create a cozy space to talk with God.
3. Read: Begin your journey by reading the Lord's Prayer (Matthew 6:9-13) in your prayer corner.
4. Arm Up: Use this area regularly to pray, talk to God, and continue building your relationship with Him, free from distractions.

ALTERNATIVE ACTIVITY:

Finish your Armor of God drawing by adding a symbol of prayer or writing the Lord's Prayer (Matthlew 6:9-13) on your drawing. Frame and hang your awesome artwork!

YOU'RE READY FOR BATTLE!
WEAR YOUR ARMOR AND KEEP IT STRONG!

REFERENCES

General Sources

- U.S. Bureau of Reclamation. (n.d.). Water facts - Worldwide water supply. Retrieved May 7, 2024, from https://www.usbr.gov/mp /arwec/water-facts-ww-water-sup.html

- Moskowitz, C. (2012, May 30). Light speed: How fast is it? Space .com. https://www.space.com/15830-light-speed.html

- Met Office. (n.d.). Moonbow. Retrieved May 5, 2024, from https://www.metoffice.gov.uk/weather/learn-about/weather/ optical-effects/rainbows/moonbow#:~:text=A%20moonbow% 20(sometimes%20known%20as,faint%20and%20very%20rarely %20seen.

- NASA Goddard Space Flight Center. (n.d.). Neutron Stars. Imagine the Universe!. Retrieved January 8, 2024, from https://imagine. gsfc.nasa.gov/science/objects/neutron_stars1.html

- National Aquarium. (n.d.). Peacock Mantis Shrimp. Retrieved January 21, 2024, from https://aqua.org/explore/animals/peacock -mantis-shrimp

- Wonderopolis. (n.d.). How many cells are in the human body? Wonderopolis. Retrieved from https://www.wonderopolis.org/ wonder/how-many-cells-are-in-the-human-body

Biblical and Historical References

- Genesis Apologetics. (n.d.). Leviathan. Retrieved from https://genesisapologetics.com/leviathan/

- Tyndale House Publishers. (n.d.). What is the Leviathan? Retrieved from https://tyndalehouse.com/explore/articles/what-is-the-leviathan/

- Woetzel, D. (2017). The Stegosaur Engravings at Ta Prohm. Answers Research Journal, 10, 213–220. https://answersresearchjournal.org/stegosaur-engravings-at-ta-prohm/.

- Institute for Creation Research. (2013, October 31). Leviathan: Legend, Croc, or Something Else? Retrieved from https://www.icr.org/article/leviathan-legend-croc-or-something-else

- Cox, G. (2022, September 29). Seven archaeological evidences for the biblical Goliath. Creation Ministries International. https://creation.com/giant-goliath-evidences

- Steinmeyer, N. (2022, November 4). Who Is Balaam Son of Beor? Part Three. Biblical Archaeology Society. https://www.biblicalarchaeology.org/daily/ancient-cultures/ancient-israel/balaam-son-of-beor-part-three/

- Ministry Magazine. (1975, April). Pontius Pilate and the Caesarea inscription. Ministry Magazine. Retrieved April 24, 2024, from https://www.ministrymagazine.org/archive/1975/04/pontius-pilate-and-the-caesarea-inscription

Videos and Multimedia

- BibleProject. (2015, June 22). The Book of Job [Video]. YouTube. https://youtu.be/PYX8cemKb6E?si=cgP3pJaJrrgEFT9u

- Jimmy Akin's Mysterious World. (2023, August 25). Flying Snakes!

[Video]. YouTube. https://youtu.be/16vDWGl_1Ck

- Tim Macie Archives. (2016, January 18). Making of the Bible (Year of Biblical Literature) [Video]. YouTube. https://youtu.be/j919U rCLbXI?si=HkH0K87EMoLbFUVP

Books and Manuscripts

- Connolly, P. (1981). Greece and Rome at war. Macdonald Phoebus.

- Goldsworthy, A. (2003). The complete Roman army. Thames & Hudson.

- Olson, M. V. (2012). Human genetic diversity and the evolution of human populations. Nature Reviews Genetics, 13(2), 89-93. https://doi.org/10.1038/nrg3115

- Josephus, F. (1981). The antiquities of the Jews (W. Whiston, Trans.). Hendrickson Publishers. (Original work published ca. 93–94 C.E.)

- Tacitus, C. (2008). The annals (A. J. Woodman, Trans.). Hackett Publishing. (Original work published ca. 116 C.E.)

- Pliny the Younger. (2003). The letters of the younger Pliny (B. Radice, Trans.). Penguin Books. (Original work published ca. 110–113 C.E.)

Images

- Castiglione, G. B. (c. 17th century). Raising of Lazarus. Public Domain. Modified to black and white.

- Shields, F. (1833–1911). Samson stands over vanquished Philistines. Public Domain. Modified to black and white.

- Delziel Brothers. (c. 19th century). Arrow of Deliverance. Public

Domain. Modified to black and white.

- The Israel Museum. (n.d.). Range: 1300–1800. Public Domain. www.imj.org.il. Modified to black and white.

- William Black. (1825). Behemoth. London: William Black. Public Domain. Modified to black and white.

- Dore, G. (c. 1866). The Creation of Light. Public Domain. Modified to black and white.

- Jan Miel. (1649–1664). Roman soldier. Rijksmuseum, Object ID: RP-P-1 5: 886-A-10472. Public Domain. Modified to black and white.

- Harald Hoyer. (2017). Dinosaur Behemoth Carving. Wikimedia Commons, CC BY-SA 2.0. https://commons.wikimedia.org/wiki/File:Dinosaur_Behemoth_Carving.jpg. Modified to black and white.

- Stockbridge, G. (1907). Elasmotherium [Photograph]. GetArchive. https://garystockbridge617.getarchive.net/amp/media/1907-500-elasmotherium-b86027. Modified to black and white.

- Lendering, J. (2007, January 28). Nabonidus Cylinder, Sippar. Wikimedia Commons. https://commons.wikimedia.org/wiki/File:Nabonidus_cylinder_sippar_bm1.jpg. Modified to black and white.

- Sauber, W. (2009, June 7). Reconstruction of a Roman centurio, Museum Quintana - Roman department. Wikimedia Commons, CC BY-SA 3.0 Unported. https://commons.wikimedia.org/wiki/File:Museum_Quintana_-_Zenturio_1.jpg. Clipped to show the breastplate and modified to black and white.

- Seré, F. (1852). Illustration from Histoire de la chaussure, depuis l'antiquité la plus reculée jusqu'à nos jours. BNF Gallica. Public

Domain. ark:/12148/bpt6k63152755

Thank You!

Thank you so much for joining me on this journey through Taking Root! I hope this devotional has brought your family closer together and strengthened your faith. Each page was crafted with love, prayer, and the hope that it would bring joy and a deeper connection with God into your daily lives.

As you move forward, remember to stay rooted in His Word, leaning on Him through every season. I pray this devotional has been a blessing and a valuable tool to guide you in that direction. Keep nurturing those roots, sharing in faith, and growing in love for one another!

If you haven't had a chance yet, please consider leaving a review to let others know about your experience with Taking Root. Your support means the world to me, and reviews make it possible for more families to discover this book and start their own journeys of growth.

Thank you again for being here. May God richly bless you and your family as you continue to grow in His Word!

With love and gratitude,

~Amy